The Fibonacci Vortex™ Handbook

by Earik Beann

Table of Contents

Chapter 1:
Introduction..4

Chapter 2:
Old Style Fibonacci Analysis...................................10

Chapter 3:
Building the Fibonacci Vortex™...........................21

Chapter 4:
The Rules..27

Chapter 5:
Scaling..41

Chapter 6:
Vortex Examples..51

Chapter 7:
Vortex Time Targets.......................................73

Chapter 8:
Vortex Price Targets.......................................82

Chapter 9:
Time and Price Squares..................................87

Chapter 10:
Integrating the Vortex into your Trading.................94

Chapter 11:
Alternative Approaches..................................103

Chapter 12:
Conclusion..115

CHAPTER ONE:
Introduction

If you've spent any time reading trading books, you've likely come across a discussion of the Fibonacci sequence. This is a simple number series first discussed in Fibonacci's (Leonardo Pisano) *Liber Abaci* (pub. 1202) which is as follows:

1, 1, 2, 3, 5, 8, 13, 21, 34, 55, 89, 144, 233, ...

To obtain the next number in the sequence, you simply add the last two. So in the series above, we start out with 1 + 1 = 2, then 1 + 2 = 3, 2 + 3 = 5, 3 + 5 = 8, and so on. The next number after what is printed would be 144 + 233 = 377.

When we divide any two consecutive numbers in this sequence, we arrive at the magic number PHI (ϕ) or 1.618. This number is an irrational number like π (3.14159...), so it has an infinite number of decimal places, but each successive number in our sequence gets closer and closer to being exact:

1/1 = 1
2/1 = 2
3/2 = 1.5
5/3 = 1.66
8/5 = 1.60
13/8 = 1.625
21/13 = 1.615
34/21 = 1.619
55/34 = 1.6176
89/55 = 1.6181
etc..

The ancient Greeks knew about this number, and felt the ratio ϕ:1 was the most aesthetically perfect proportion. They tried to work this ratio into their art and architecture in as many ways as possible, and because of this, ϕ:1 soon became known as the *Golden Ratio.*

More important than the Greeks is that these numbers show up everywhere in the natural world. For example, if you take the seed pattern in a sunflower, you will find that it consists of two spirals moving in opposite directions. More specifically 21 seeds going one way, and 34 going the other. These are consecutive numbers in our number sequence as given above. A pine cone has spirals of 5 and 8 petals, also numbers from our sequence. A pineapple has 8 and 13. Flower petals, branching plants, shells, seeds, leaves, and countless other things all grow according to these numbers.

This number also appears many times in the human body. If you take a look at your own hands, you will see:

2 hands, each of which has…
5 fingers, each of which has…
3 sections, divided by…
2 knuckles

Not only that, the ratio of the longest bone in a finger to the next smaller bone in the finger is approximately 1.618. So even our hands are based on this growth ratio.

We can show this growth ratio graphically in the following way. Take a square, with sides equal to 1 unit. Now, create progressively larger squares based on enlarging previous squares by the golden ratio, and then arrange them like this:

First square:

Next one:

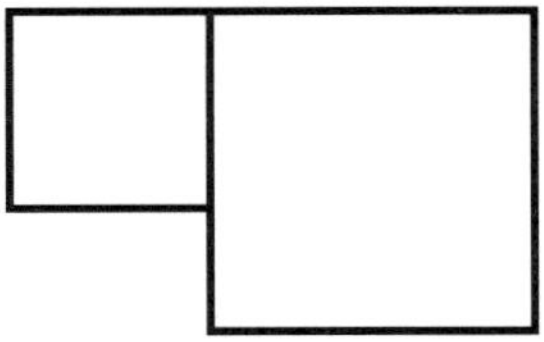

Again:

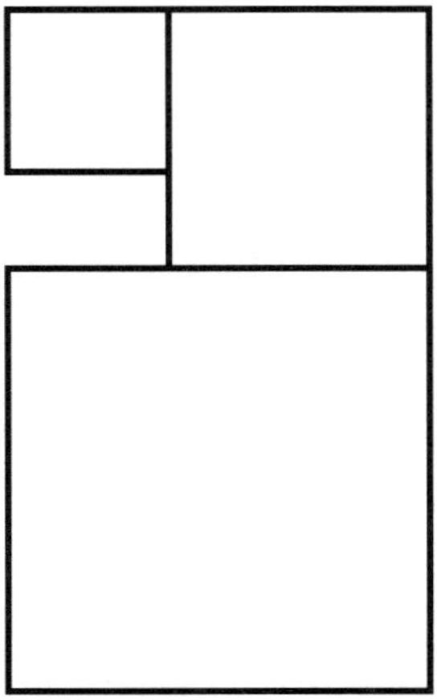

Note that just like our Fibonacci sequence, the third square's width is the equal to the sum of the two that came before it. Additionally, it is 1.618 times as large as the square that came immediately before it.

Once more:

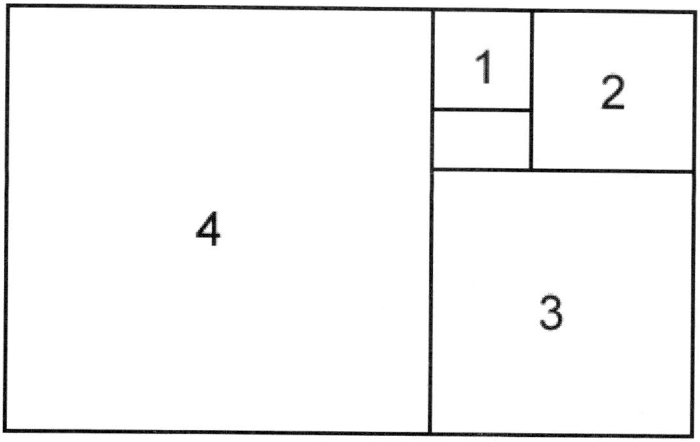

You can visually see how the numbers add up. Square number 3 is the same width as squares 1+2, and square number 4 is the same as squares 2+3.

finally, we can put quarter-circles inside the square to get this:

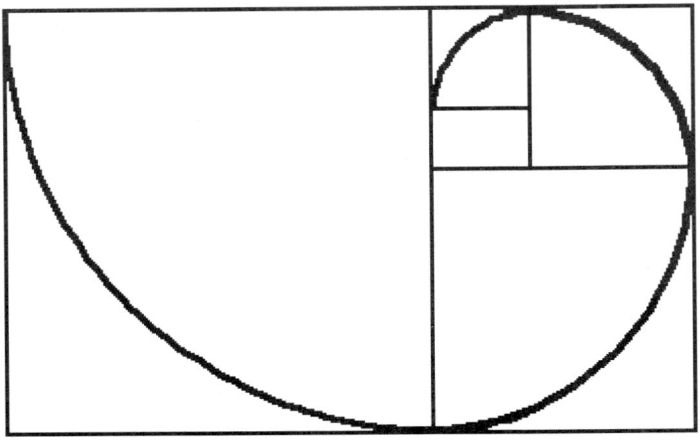

This process has created *Golden Rectangles*, which in turn created a *Golden Spiral*. The Golden Spiral is the basis for such shapes as the Nautilus shell and even the Milky Way. So even galaxies follow this growth pattern.

As traders, when we stumble upon something so fundamental and basic to the natural world, it usually pays to give that law our undivided attention. Markets are reflections of mass psychology, so any kind of patterns that govern us also must show up in the market.

The market is not made up of random numbers, as many academics would have us believe. Benoit Mandelbrot, the father of Chaos Theory, proved mathematically that markets were not random, and successful traders worldwide prove it every day with their consistent profits.

To many traders, the market is a living, breathing entity, and the patterns it forms are just as beautiful and regular as the patterns we find in the sunflowers and seashells. More importantly, the market follows the same natural laws as everything else, so studying the patterns of the universe will also bear fruit when applied to a study of the patterns of the market.

This book details the discovery and application of one such pattern. It is a geometrical pattern based on the number sequences we have been discussing here, and unlike most other Fibonacci applications, can give you both time *and* price targets of market turns well in advance. I have named this pattern the Fibonacci Vortex™.

In my opinion, it is one of the greatest support and resistance tools available to traders. In this book you'll learn what the vortex is, how to apply it, and most importantly, how to trade it. It is my belief that markets are constructed by the mass consciousness using building blocks based on components of the Fibonacci Vortex pattern. This is a strong statement to make, but after reading this book, it is my hope that you will agree with me.

CHAPTER TWO:
Old Style Fibonacci Analysis

As the Vortex is based on Fibonacci, it is helpful to understand some of the more standard approaches to using Fibonacci in market analysis. This chapter will provide a quick overview of the classic methods that traders use to analyze markets with Fibonacci numbers.

The idea behind using Fibonacci to analyze markets is based in the fact that Fibonacci numbers govern growth processes in the natural world. As plants and animals grow, their bodies follow rules based on Fibonacci relationships. Markets, while not alive, also are constantly growing and changing.

A bull market begins as a seed just at the end of a bear market. It sprouts up from the ground with the first impulse wave, breaking old highs and reversing the losses that had battered the stock down during the previous decline. Like a plant, it grows bit by bit until it has a fully developed and mature form.

The patterns that the market exhibits while growing are always different, yet always similar. Just as we know a plant goes from seed, to sprout, to sapling, to full grown tree, we know a market will go from impulse wave, to consolidation, to impulse, in a relatively orderly way.

As Fibonacci ratios define how things grow in the natural world, and allow us to measure the extent of this growth, it is a logical step to try and apply them to market growth. To determine how far a market will move (and when it will turn around and go the other way), is of course the ultimate goal of any analyst.

The most basic method of applying Fibonacci to markets is in simple ratio analysis. In this form of analysis, we take the price distance of the last swing, measure it, then multiply by 1.618 to determine the price distance we expect the very next swing to travel. We can also multiply by relatives of Phi, to obtain an entire range of price targets.

There are whole books written about this technique, so I won't go into too much detail about the various ratios that can be used. In the examples below, I'll keep things simple, and use the following two ratios:

$$\mathbf{1.618} = \phi$$
$$\mathbf{0.618} = \mathbf{1} / \phi$$

Take a look at the following chart of IBM:

IBM has recently completed an upswing and now looks to be topping off. We can measure the distance between the low and the high, multiply by 0.618 and 1.618, and project back down from the recent high to obtain possible support levels.

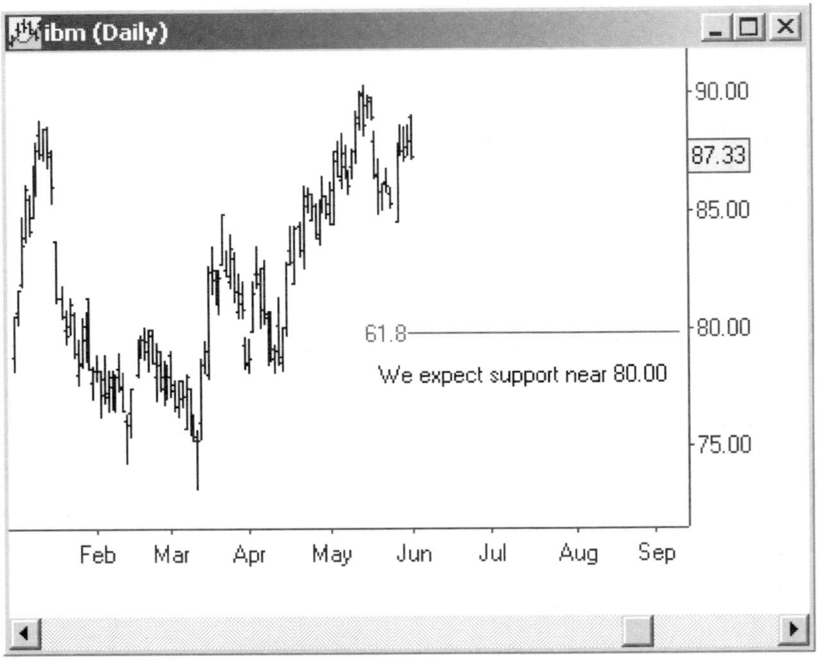

The chart above shows this approach in action. Now, as the market declines, we can monitor this level for a possible signal to add to our long positions. For clarification, note that the chart shows this level as a percentage, so 0.618 is the same as 61.8%.

Here's what happened:

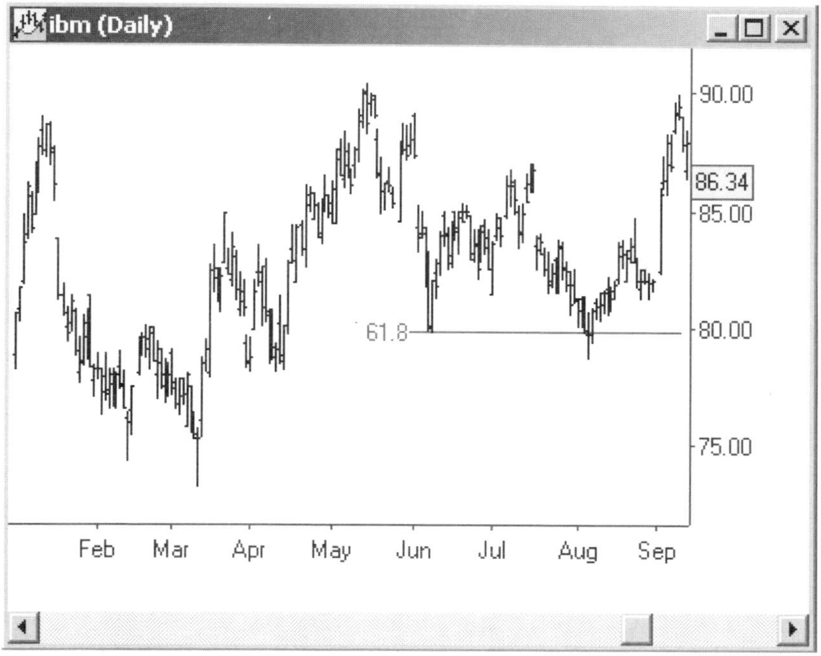

The market came down hard, stopped on our 0.618 level (to the cent) and then rallied. It re-tested the level a couple months later before finally continuing on to break above the May highs.

This is just a single example, but you can see it happening over and over if you watch for it. I personally know professional traders that use this very basic technique combined with price patterns as their primary form of analysis, and it works very well for them.

Here are a couple more examples from IBM:

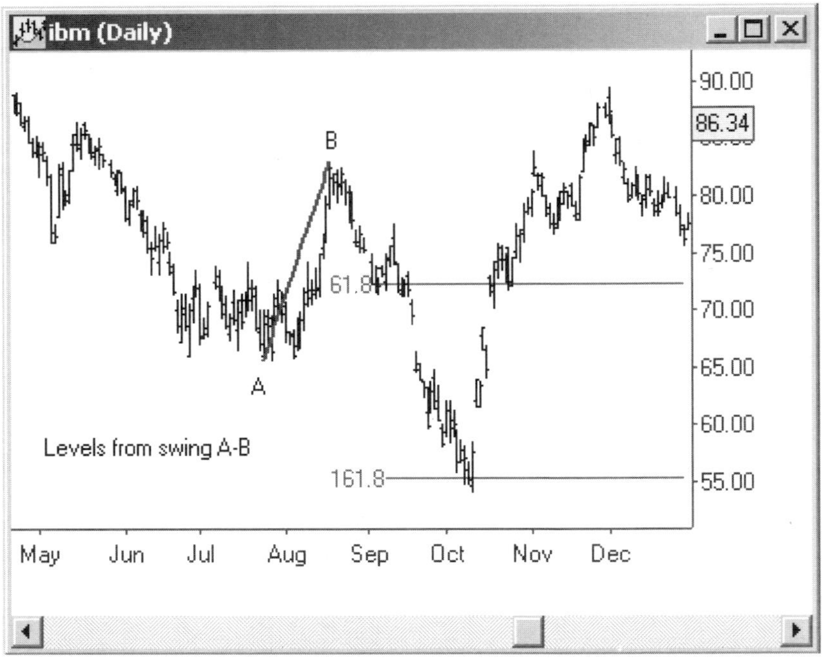

This chart shows ratio analysis of the swing marked A-B. Note that the market paused right at the 0.618 level before entering a free-fall into the lower 1.618 level, which it was unable to break.

The next chart shows two levels from different swing points acting as a loose cluster. The 0.618 level from swing A-C was a little low, but the 1.618 level from B-C was just right. Together, they marked the top of the rally and the beginning of a second decline.

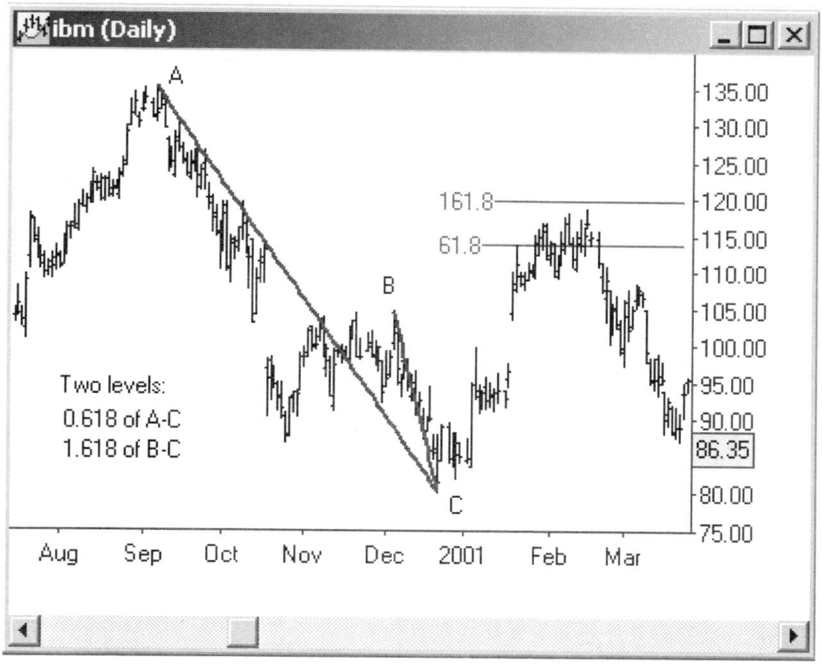

We can do a similar form of analysis using time. So instead of measuring the price distance from a bottom to top and projecting future price levels, we can measure the time distance from those same two points to project a future time zone where we expect a turning point to form.

We use the same ratios, only this time we're going to examine the time axis instead of the price axis. Let's take a look at an example:

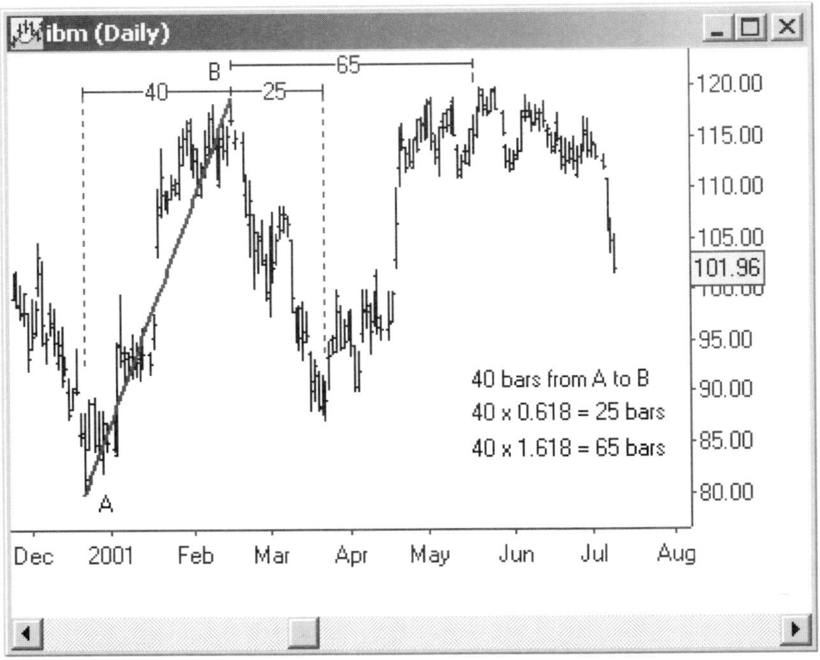

In this chart, I've measured the time it took to move from the low at point A to the high at point B. This is 40 bars. Now, multiply by our ratios to get:

40 bars x 0.618 = 24.72 bars (round to 25)

and

40 bars x 1.618 = 64.72 bars (round to 65)

Then, project these bar counts from point B to get future turns. You can see that 25 bars later we had a reaction low, and 65 bars later we had a top. The low was exact to the bar, and the top was off by two days.

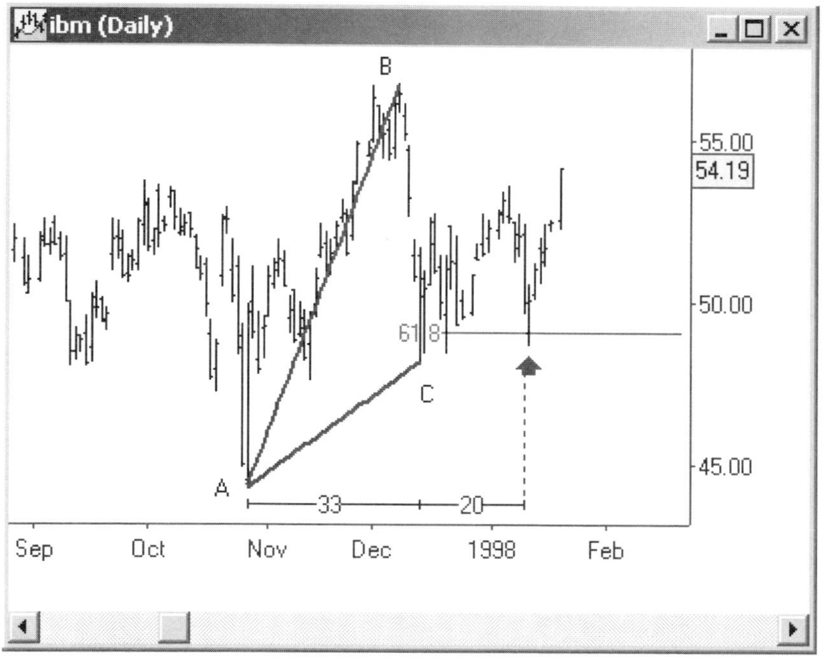

The chart above shows a combination of both techniques. First, we get our price target by measuring the swing A-B and multiplying by 0.618. Next, we take the time distance from A-C (not a swing, but two important lows) and multiply by 0.618. You'll note that the market bottomed at a spot where both time and price came together. This location is shown on the chart by the arrow. It was off of the ideal by one day and around 30 cents, so it was very accurate.

Generally, the signals from this type of analysis are much stronger when you have both time and price components acting together as in this last example.

There are many other methods that have been used to apply these ratios to market action, but these examples should be enough to give you a good idea what it's all about. It can be very accurate at times, but there are a few drawbacks to this simple style of analysis:

The first drawback is that we don't really know how long a particular support/resistance level is valid for. On the chart above, we have seen the market bottom out on these levels right after a big drop. But after this happens, is the level still valid? What happens if the market never touches a level, but comes back to it years later? In that case, can we trust the level, or has it's strength faded with time? If so, is there a way to measure the fading strength of a level so that we know which ones to trust and which ones to ignore?

I don't have a definitive answer to those questions. Sometimes you can use older lines, especially if they are based off of major swing points. Other times, you just watch as the market passes right through old lines without a pause.

A second problem with this form of analysis is that it can easily lead to using a huge amount of ratios. I've only looked at two different levels, 1.618 and 0.618, but the proponents of this style of analysis often use many more. You can multiply 0.618 by itself to get the ratio 0.382, which is important, so that should be used, and don't forget the square root value of 0.786! Now we're up to four levels in a very short amount of time, and there are many more that I haven't mentioned.

If you look in the tool box of most popular software packages, you'll likely see a Fibonacci Retracements tool in there somewhere. It usually plots around 10 different levels, running out all the way to 4.235 (1.618 x 1.618 x 1.618) and beyond. When you apply this kind of tool to multiple swing measurements, you get into analysis overload very quickly. There are often just too many lines on the screen to follow with any confidence! This is probably the biggest criticism of ratio analysis. If you put enough lines on a chart, you're bound to hit highs and lows somewhere.

Finally, this method of analysis breaks the chart down into separate price and time components, which is not necessarily a good thing to do. A chart with no time element is not going to be very useful. And a chart with no price element is going to be very flat. In short, the time and price elements of the chart are interdependent and should ideally be used together instead of separately.

The market is not a one-dimensional construct, and should not be treated as such. Just as a plant lives in three dimensions with length, width, and height, so does a market live with time and price. It is useless to know the price of a stock without also knowing when it was at that price, so the two pieces of information go hand in hand.

While this doesn't mean that we *can't* break the chart into two separate components as we've done in the examples above, it does raise a few philosophical issues about the approach which ought to be considered.

Of course, in trading no one cares about philosophy for it's own sake. We all want results, and we'll use the tools that work the best no matter how they are calculated. However, the consideration of the relationship between time and price is what partially lead to the discovery of the Fibonacci Vortex, and when it comes to results, this tool leaves the older methods far in the dust. So in this case, trying to keep the time and price axes united paid some huge dividends.

Not only does the Vortex overcome the drawbacks of the standard methods as mentioned above, it does so with increased accuracy and clarity. You know exactly when a resistance level is valid and for how long. You also know when the Vortex has lost strength and no longer has any effect on market action. And, best of all, you know where the support and resistance levels are located in both time *and* price, not just in one or the other.

So with that much of introduction and background, I'll leave the discussion of the older tools to others, and move on into a more detailed look at what the Fibonacci Vortex is and how we can use it to improve our trading results.

CHAPTER THREE:
Building the Fibonacci Vortex™

The Fibonacci Vortex is a complex pattern built on the basic Fibonacci building blocks that we discussed in chapter one. As we have seen in that chapter, we can create a graphical depiction of the Fibonacci sequence using squares in a spiral form. This process creates the Golden Spiral:

This pattern is very important in nature, and has captivated the minds of scientists and philosophers throughout history. Issac Newton was so taken with this shape that he had it carved into his bedframe. Even farther back, the Egyptians build their pyramids in such a way that if you look at them from space, you would see that they are all connected along the path of a Fibonacci spiral.

Note that the spiral above begins in the center, and spirals out to the right. Let's add another spiral to this, beginning at the center and then spiraling left:

Now we have two spirals, connected at the center point. This is one half of our pattern. Remember, it's just two Golden Spirals connected at the origin.

We also need to look at the spirals that move in the opposite direction:

This is an upside down version of the spiral pair shown earlier. To construct this by hand, you actually only need one spiral drawn out on a clear plastic overlay. Then you just flip and rotate as needed to get the four directions.

The next step is to combine all four spirals into a single pattern:

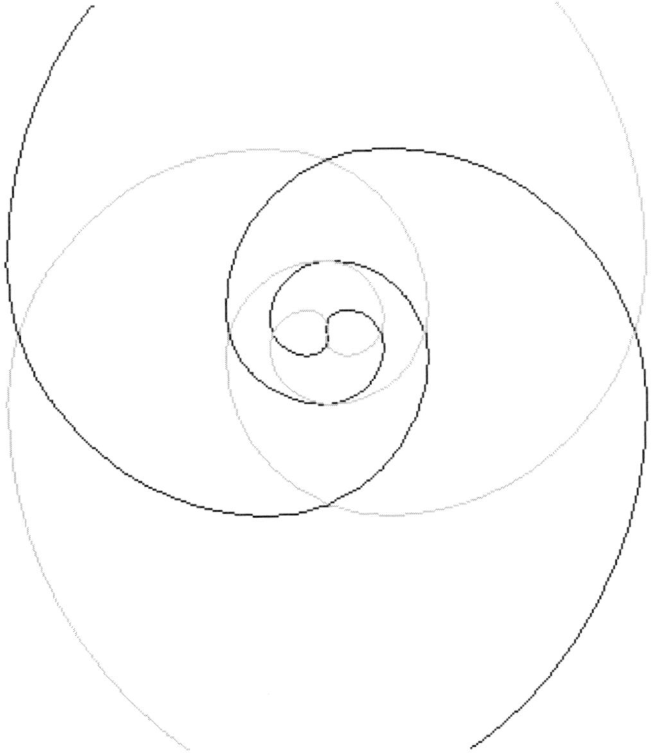

I think you'll begin to appreciate why this is called a vortex pattern. We have four Golden Spirals, connected at a single point. You'll note that one pair of spirals is darker than the other. This helps us tell the spirals apart, which is going to be important later on when we start applying this pattern to charts.

There is one last step that we need to do before our vortex is complete. If you look at the pattern above, you can see that everything comes together at the center. If these spirals represented waves of energy traveling out from a fixed point, they would come together periodically as each spiral crossed the other in it's path outward from the source. These intersection points are called nodes, and you can see them directly above, below, to the right, and to the left of this pattern. In short, you have a node when the darker spiral crosses over the lighter one.

These nodal points are important because they represent locations where there is energy present from both spirals at the same time. After examining this pattern on countless price charts, I discovered that price respects the nodal energy. Not only at the node itself, but anywhere along a line connecting a node to the center.

Let's put those into our pattern now:

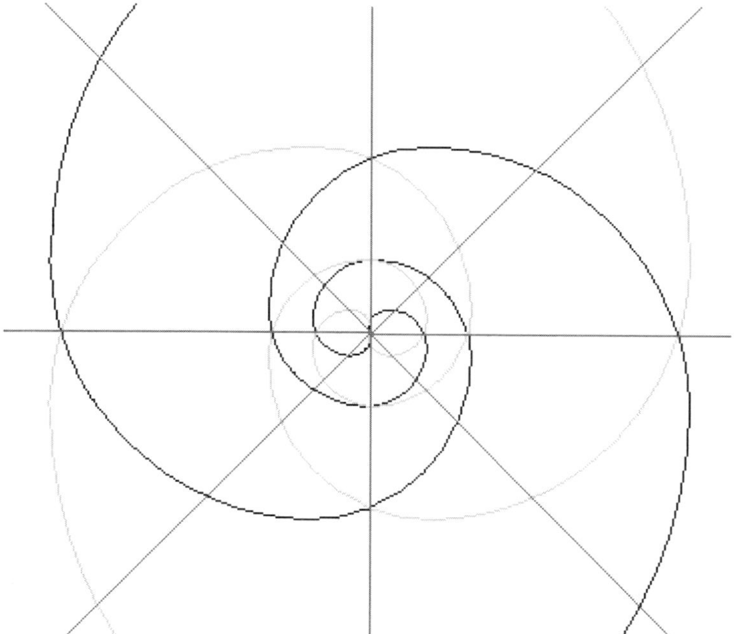

So now we have lines running from the center through the nodes. These are shown as the vertical and horizontal lines on the graphic above. We also have lines drawn at the midpoint between the nodes. These are shown as the diagonal lines. All of them are important, and collectively are known as the spokes.

So this is the complete Fibonacci Vortex pattern, consisting of four spirals and eight spokes. Using the information provided in chapter one about how to construct a Golden Spiral, along with the instructions in this chapter, you should now be able to construct this pattern from scratch, using only a compass and ruler. You might not want to, but you *could* if you had to. Luckily for us, we have computers that can do it much faster and without any complaining.

CHAPTER FOUR:
The Rules

Now that we know what the Fibonacci Vortex is, it's time to learn how to use it. In this chapter, I'm going to discuss the best way I've found to do so. It consists of two parts:

1) **Sizing the Vortex**
2) **Projecting Support/Resistance**

Since the Vortex is a geometrical pattern, it can have many different sizes. We can have tiny vortexes for minute patterns on a 1 minute chart, as well as giant vortexes that span years and years on a monthly chart. Both look exactly the same, but are built using different squares when constructing the initial Golden Spirals.

Before we can do anything, we need to find a vortex that will be the correct size for the chart we are analyzing. The market gets to determine what size vortex we use, so we need to get this information directly from the price chart itself:

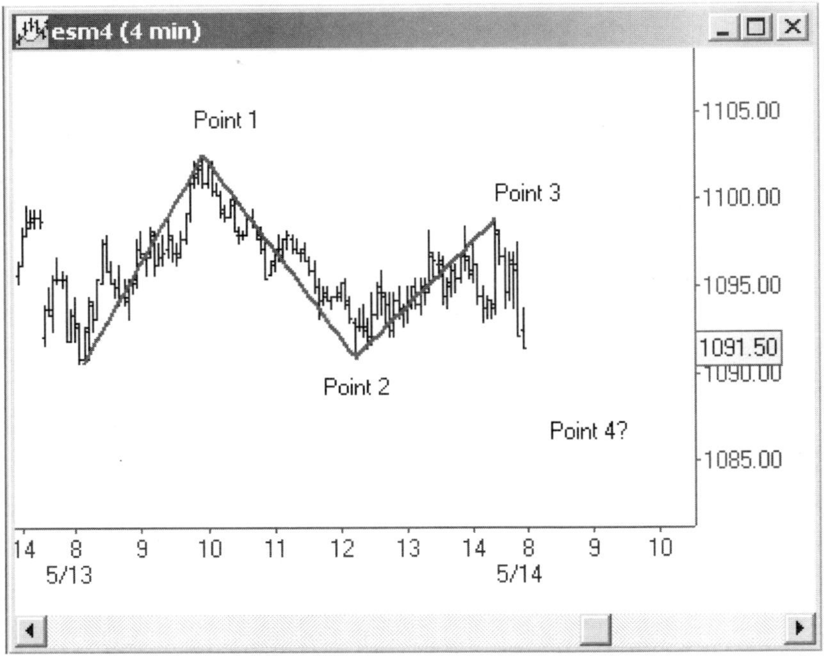

What we need to do first is identify the last three important swing highs and lows. In the chart above, I've marked them as Point 1, Point 2, and Point 3. We moved from the high at Point 1, down to a low at Point 2, then back up to the latest swing high at Point 3. What we are going to try to do is use our Vortex to figure out where Point 4 will come in.

The next step after finding our swing points is to place our vortex so that it's center is on the extreme high or low of Point 3. Since Point 3 on the chart above is a swing high, we'll place the Vortex at the high price of this bar.

I'll do that now:

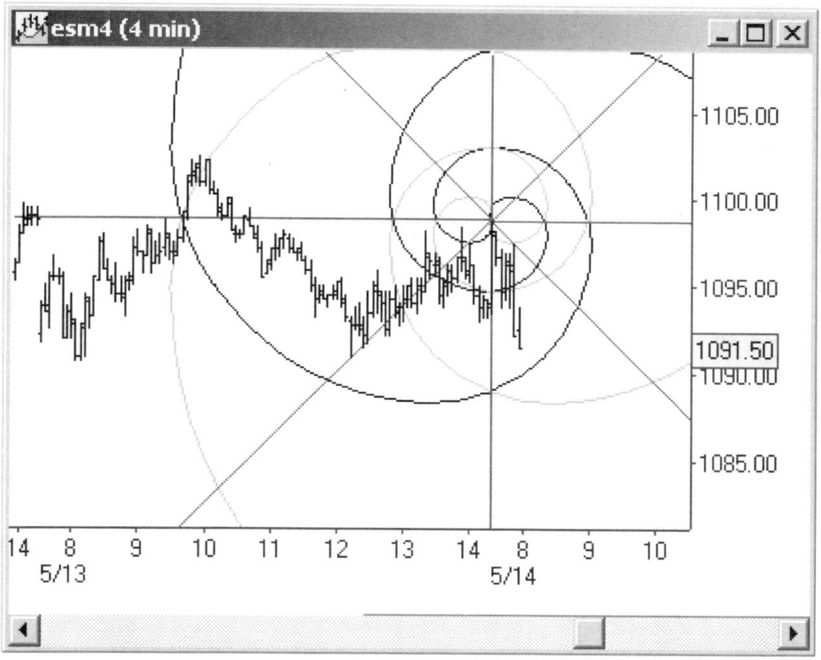

Now we need to use Points 1 and 2 to help us size our Vortex. Our goal is to have one of the spirals passing through Point 2, and one of the spokes passing through Point 1. This is the criteria for finding the correct vortex to use for our three swing points. If the current vortex doesn't fit, then we have to try a larger vortex and see if it does. We go on in this way until we find a match.

Remember to start off with the small vortex and work your way up to the larger ones. We want to find the smallest vortex we can that meets our criteria.

Let's begin:

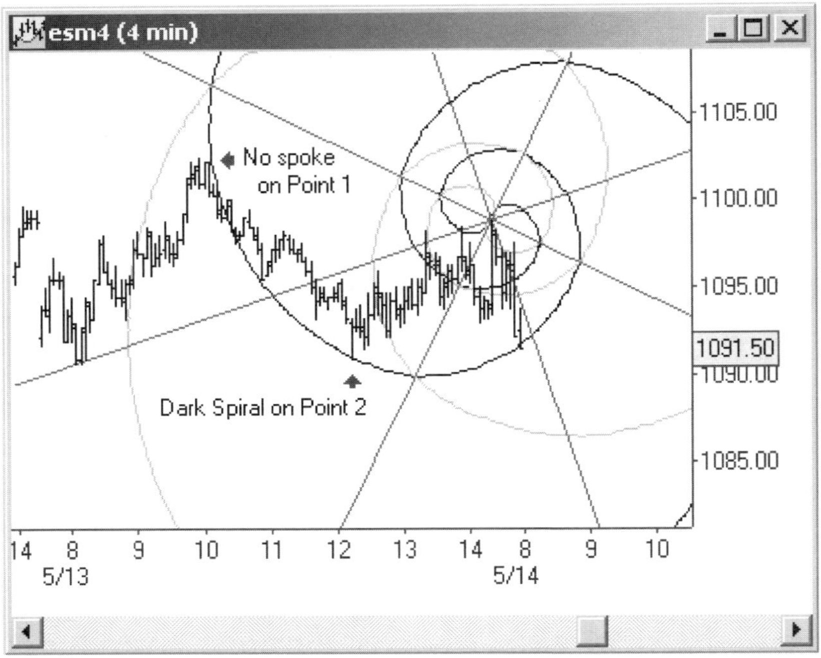

I've rotated the vortex so that the dark spiral passes exactly through the low at Point 2, but there is no spoke anywhere near Point 1. So there's no match.

Now we have to check to see what happens when we place the lighter spiral on Point 2:

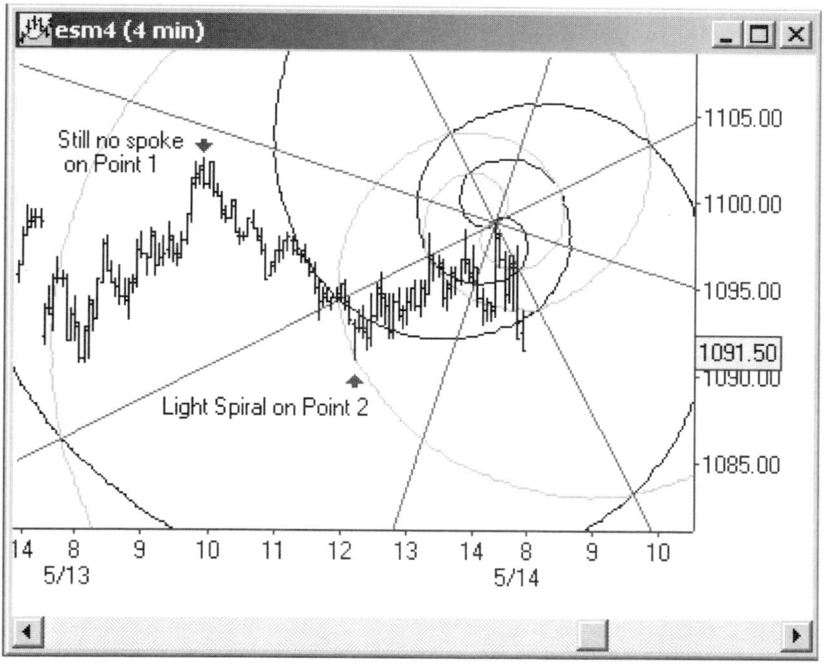

The lighter spiral is now set to pass through Point 2, but there is still no spoke on point 1. This means that we are using the wrong Vortex for these three points. We need to increase the size and try the next larger Vortex to see if it matches.

When increasing, I usually go to a Vortex that is 10% larger than the last. This means that if you built your first pattern using an initial square that was 1" x 1", you should move to a larger pattern that was built with an initial square of around 1.1" x 1.1".

Let's increase:

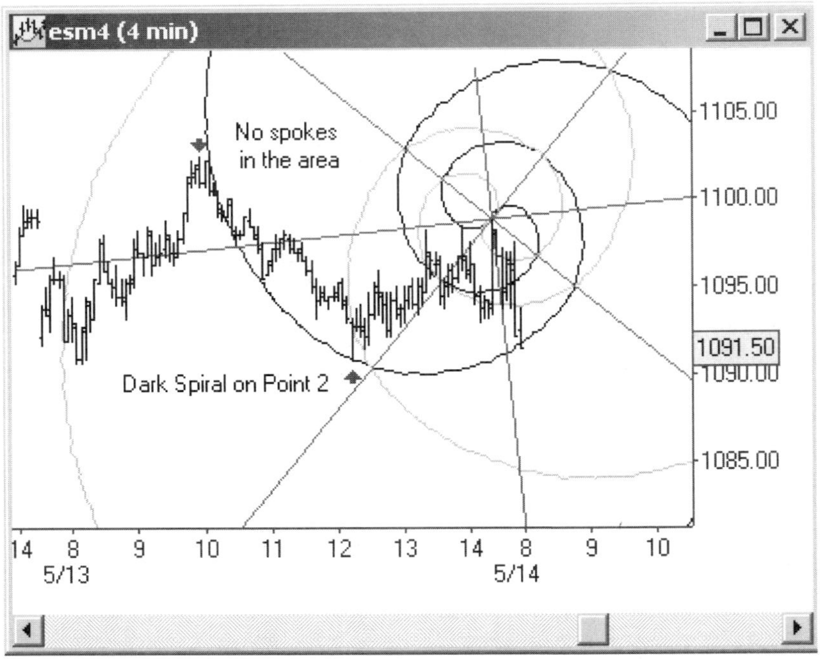

We now have a larger vortex set with the dark spiral passing through Point 2. Unfortunately, there are no spokes to be seen anywhere near Point 1.

Let's try the light spiral on Point 2:

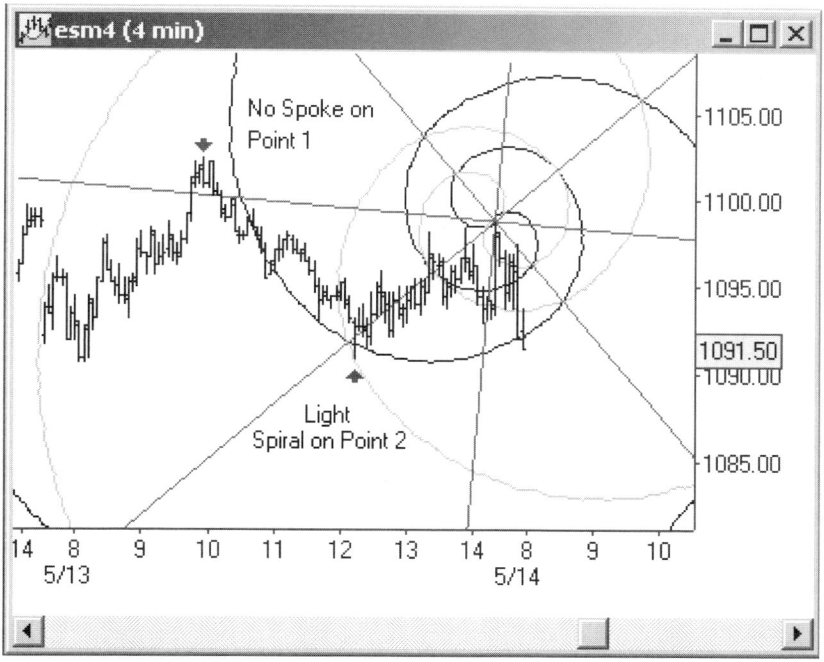

This is getting closer, but is still not right. Remember, we need to be as exact as possible when sizing the vortex. Although there can be a little slop here and there, you ideally want everything to be exact. You shouldn't really see any space between the spirals/spokes and the swing points.

Since this Vortex is not a fit, we need to increase the size and try again. I think the process is clear though, so I'll just jump to the end to show the correct fit:

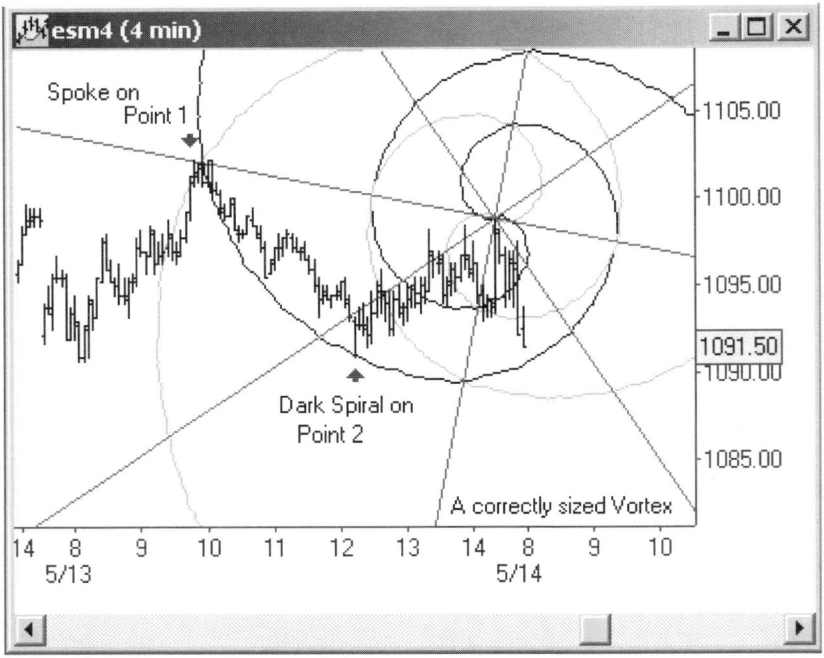

This is a correctly sized Vortex pattern. We have the center of our Vortex on Point 3, a spiral running through Point 2, and a spoke touching Point 1. Notice how exact everything is. This is what you need to do to find the right size pattern to use.

Now that we have the correct size pattern, we can move to the second stage where we use it to locate support and resistance. In this stage, we just watch for price to bounce off one of our spirals. It will look something like this:

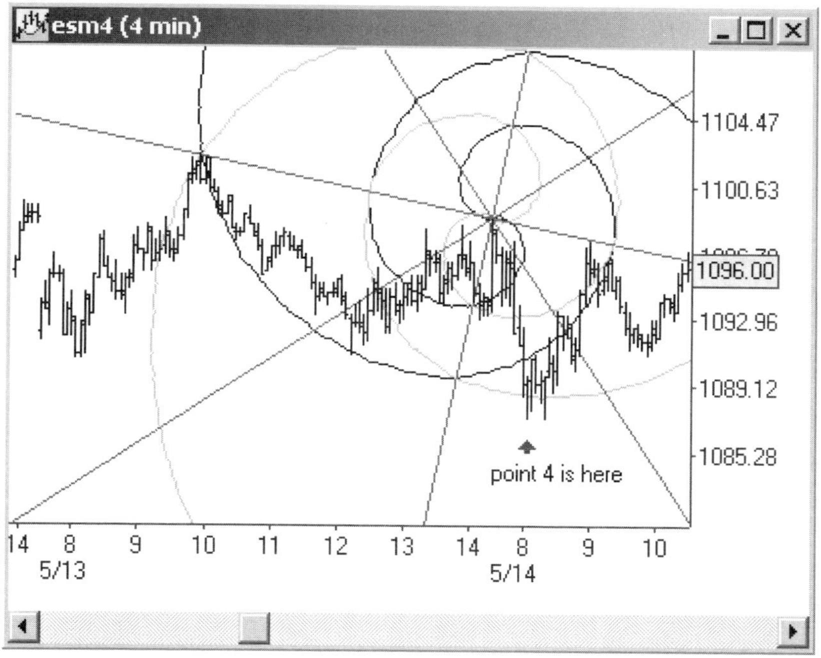

You can see that price dropped into the light spiral, which it was not able to close beneath.

There's one other thing that you need to know when looking into the future. You have to watch the Vortex pattern you just found, but you also have to watch the same pattern with the other spiral passing through Point 2.

Markets are chaotic systems, and chaotic systems always have at least two solutions. This is why the cycle traders always find that their forecasts invert on them. It is no different here. Once you find the correct size, you have one match already. Then just rotate the spiral so the other color spoke runs through Point 2 and check that as well. Both vortexes will be active at the same time.

No need to worry about spokes hitting Point 1 at this stage. That was just to help size the pattern. Once it's sized, just remember to watch both patterns.

In the example above, here's what the other Vortex looked like:

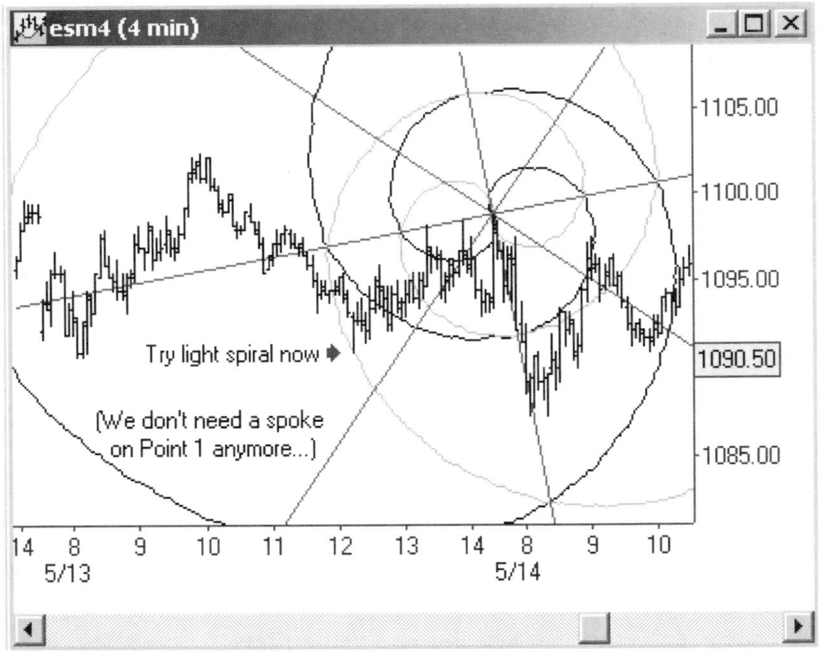

So this is the other vortex, with the light spiral passing through Point 2 instead of the dark one. It would have come into play had price broken through the spiral on our first pattern and continued down.

This may seem like a lot of trouble to apply this pattern, but don't worry – it gets very easy after you do it a few times. I use this pattern on a 1 minute S&P chart, and can slap it up and size it without feeling rushed at all. It's just a matter of practice.

To recap:

Find the Correct Size Vortex using 3 Points

1) Center of Vortex on Point 3
2) Spiral on Point 2
3) Spoke on Point 1

Start off with the smallest pattern, and check the above criteria. Keep increasing the size of the pattern until the requirements are satisfied. Remember to test both dark and light spirals on Point 2.

Projecting the Vortex

1) Vortex with dark spiral through Point 2
2) Vortex with light spiral through Point 2

Make sure to watch both of these vortex patterns together. Either one can mark the turn. (Information in later chapters will help you decide which vortex is the right one.)

For completeness, let's take a look at one more example where our second spiral was the one that caught the turn.

Below is a two minute chart with marked swings:

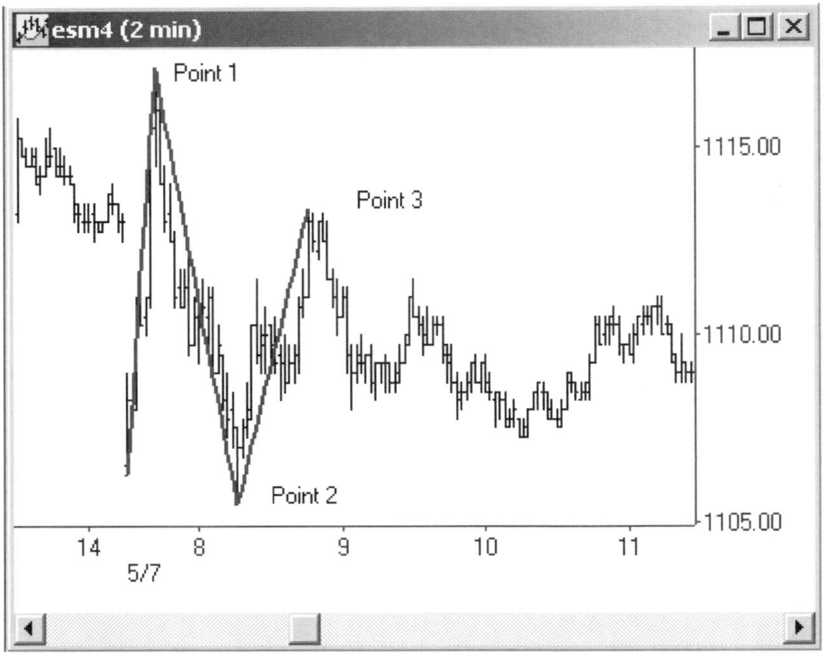

So the next step is to place our vortex on Point 3, and size it so that a spiral runs through Point 2, and a spoke through Point 1. We look for the smallest pattern we can find where these conditions are true.

It will look like this:

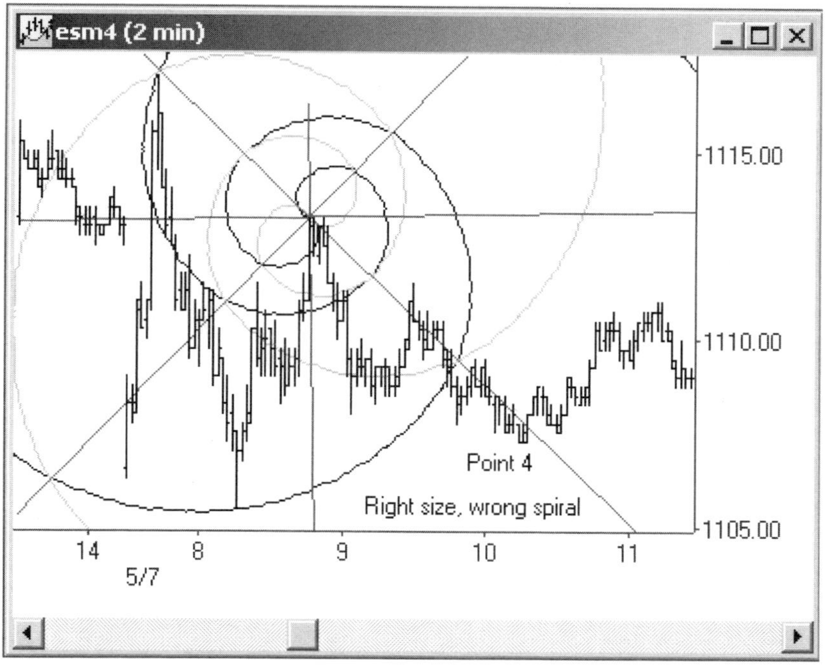

You can see we have the correct size vortex here. The dark spiral is running through the low at Point 2, and we have a spoke resting on the high at Point 1.

However, no support is shown at the bottom at Point 4. That's because this vortex only represents half the picture. We also need to keep an eye on the one with the light spiral through Point 2.

Take a look:

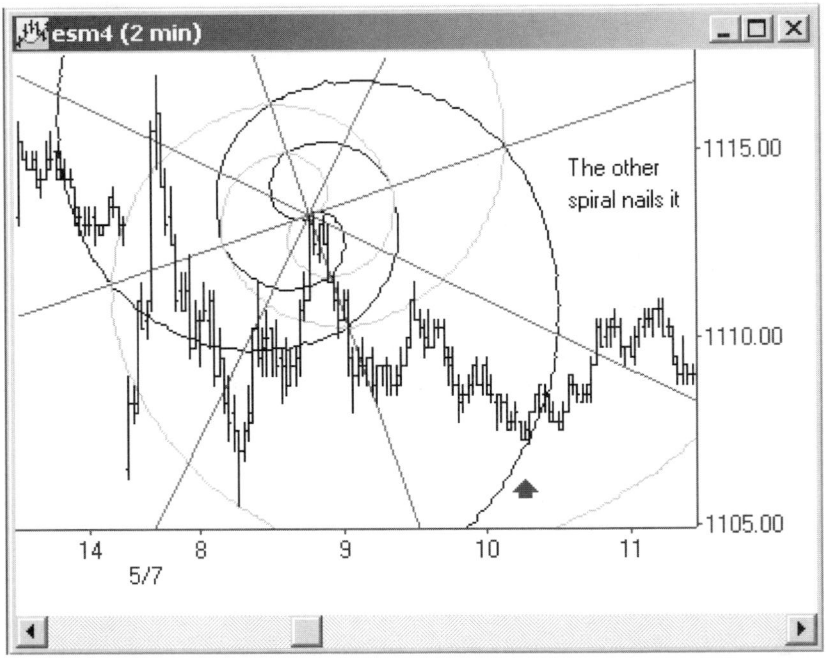

Using this vortex with the light spiral through Point 2 did the trick! We got the low at the arrow to the tick.

In this chapter, we've gone over how to size a vortex and use it to locate support and resistance levels in the future. Make sure you understand the process to find the correct size vortex pattern. Anytime we use the vortex on a chart, we need to make sure we've got the correct one. It's like cutting a piece of wood. If you go and grab the hammer instead of the saw, you're not going to have the greatest results. So make sure you size your vortex as accurately as you can before using it in your analysis.

CHAPTER FIVE:
Scaling

Now that you know how to size a vortex, it's time to shift gears and talk about scaling the chart. This is a critically important concept that is strangely missing in the published trading literature. Without proper chart scaling, the vortex (and any other geometric pattern) will not work.

There are two axes on a chart, one for price and the other for time. You need to know about both to make any sense out of what the chart means. If you think about it, all a chart really describes is a history of how price moved through time. So at the very basic level, these two things are intimately related.

It actually goes farther than that. Legendary traders like WD Gann found that price and time are really different measurements of the same thing. Once you know how it works, you can easily convert from one to the other.

I'll give a simple example of this:

In the chart above, IBM made a low at 54.00 in the middle of October. We take this number, then just count forward 54 degrees of movement of the Sun, and we get the top in December. Accuracy was within one day. The Sun is the true time keeper, and is more accurate than a bar count, which is why I'm using it here.

So in this case, *price* is giving us *time*. This would not be possible if the two weren't related. Is this just a hand-picked example? Take a look at what IBM did after just after this top:

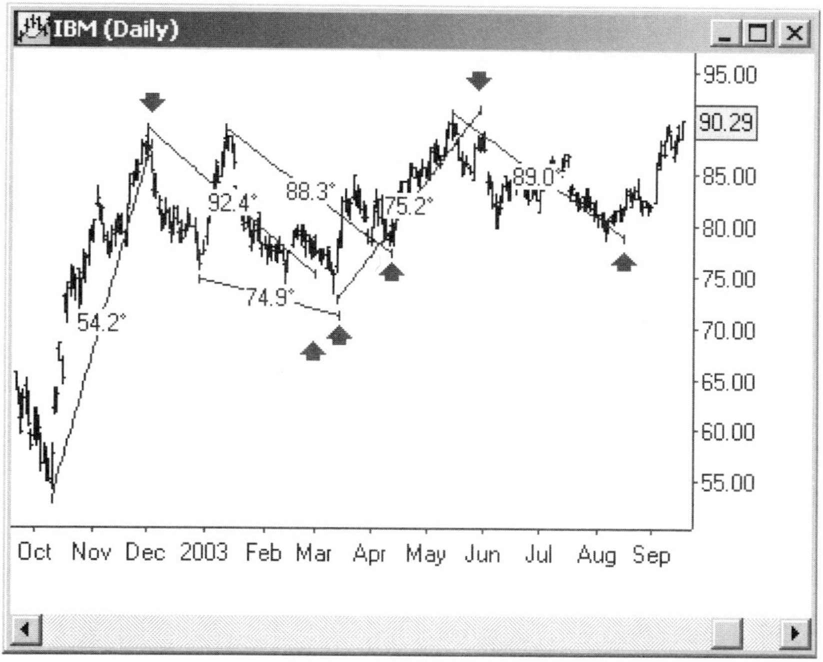

Each count on the chart is simply converting the price of the high or low to degrees, then projecting forward. The arrows show the turning points that were caught using this extremely basic technique. Not bad for a technique that is supposedly working on two totally unrelated variables…

Once we realize that there is a connection between price and time, it becomes clear that we should try and construct our charts to reflect this relationship in as best a way as we can. We do this by scaling the chart so that time and price move in fixed harmonic ratios.

All the legendary traders like Gann, Bayer, and Marechal knew about scaling their charts. Since they drew their charts by hand, they were actually forced to think about scaling right from the beginning. Only recently with the advent of computer charting software have traders gotten away from this practice. Most software programs automatically scale the chart so that price just fits the entire page. It makes sense if you're a computer programmer, and it looks nice, but it's the death of any patterns that might be hidden in that price chart. I actually had to go and write my own software so I'd be able to do this kind of analysis in real time.

So when we scale a chart, what we do is come up with an exchange rate between price and time. This is called a scale factor. The simplest scale factor is just one point per bar.

What this means is that the width of one bar on the chart is the same as the width of one point. I call this square scaling, because one unit of price and one unit of time are the same measurement, forming a square. If we had a scale of one point per bar, and our chart was 50 bars wide, then our price axis would have to be 50 points high. Once you know the scale, you can take out a ruler and verify that they are exactly the same length.

An amazing thing happens when a chart is properly scaled. All of a sudden all kinds of patterns start jumping out. You can find squares, circles, and triangles scattered throughout the price chart. These patterns would be invisible on an automatically scaled computer chart, but they are clear as day once the scaling is set properly.

The difference between a properly scaled chart and an improperly scaled chart can be immense. Let me give you an example:

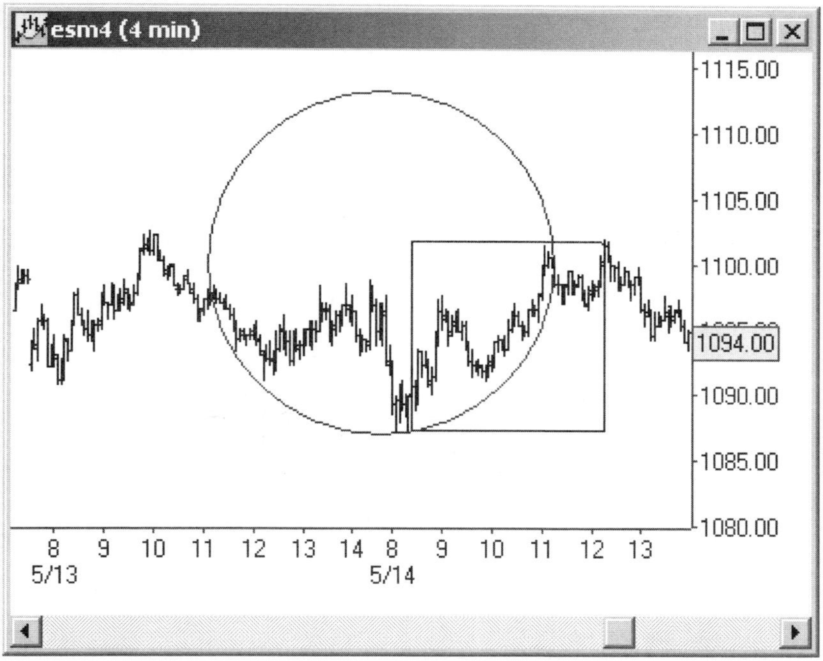

The chart above is a 4 minute chart scaled at 0.25 points per bar. Notice how the simple shapes of a circle and a square do a very good job of defining price action. It wasn't difficult to find these patterns – any scaled chart will exhibit countless geometric patterns like this.

Now let's take a look at a chart without any scaling:

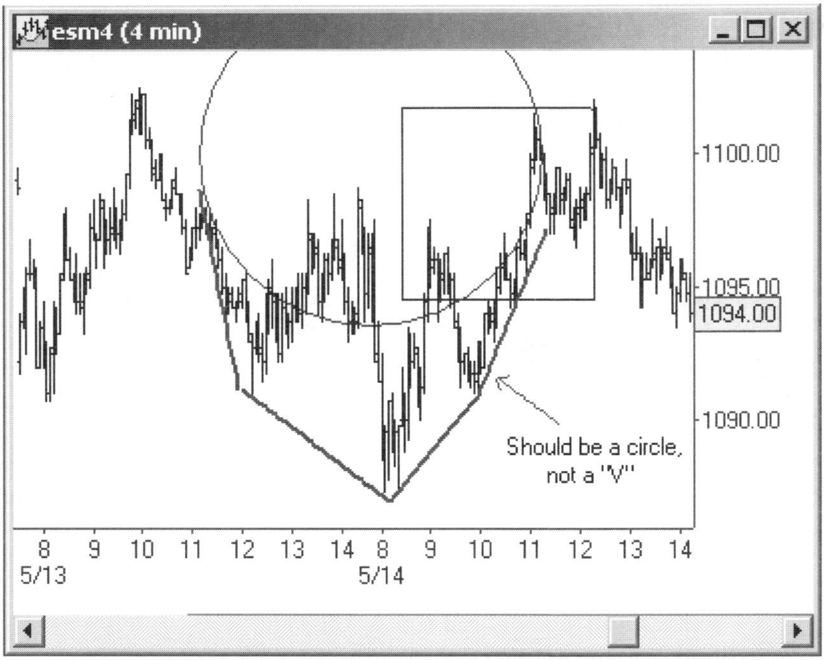

This chart is drawn using automatic computer scaling, which is pretty much how all the "industry standard" software programs work today. That square is just not cutting it anymore. It's just too short. And our circle is hurting too. I've drawn lines to show where the circle should be hitting, but no circle is going to be able to contort itself to fit into that wedge shape. What we've basically done is lost all geometry that was on the chart. Any shape that we might find in this situation will be based on random luck, and will not be reliable for trading.

If you wonder why most commercial software doesn't offer geometric patterns like the Vortex, the reason is because these patterns don't work on improperly scaled charts, which the developers insist on having. So the result is the patterns are just ignored all together, and the focus falls entirely on oscillators like Stochastics and RSI. Good luck trying to make any money using just oscillators! Better to unplug the computer and shoot for minimum wage somewhere – at least there will be a positive cash flow flipping burgers, which is something you're not going to be able to say about those oscillators.

Scale your charts and a whole new realm of analysis will open it's doors to you. Shapes will appear everywhere, your Gann angles will start to work like they're supposed to, and price and time will start to tell a story. That story will give you a huge edge over the traders that don't scale their charts, because you can see it and they cannot.

So now that we've discussed the importance of scaling a chart, the question arises as to how we can find the right scale for our particular market and time frame.

Unfortunately, there isn't a formula that you can just plug values into that gives back a scale factor in return. You've got to hunt down the correct scale factor by examining the chart and looking for the settings that work. The one good thing about scale factors is that once you find one that works, it will keep working forever. They are extremely stable.

The process I recommend for finding a scale factor on a market is the following:

1) Find a scale factor that makes the market look "right".

The human brain is built to find patterns. When you scale your chart properly and the patterns show up, your subconscious is going to like it. Scaled charts always look good to the naked eye.

So just eyeball the numbers until you get something that looks close. If 1 point per day is too steep, try half a point or a quarter point per day instead. Keep fooling with it until you get in range.

Once you find something that looks good, you can check it by going to the next step:

2) Look for geometric patterns in the price chart

Once you have a potential scale factor, go through the chart and see how many perfect circles you can find. A properly scaled chart will have many circles everywhere. Remember, price has to touch the circle in at least three different spots for it to be genuine.

If your scale is close, but not quite right, then the market will just be slightly off of your circles. We're looking to be as exact as possible here.

Also look for other shapes such as squares and triangles. Those will be present as well. And don't forget the Fibonacii Vortex itself. Try it out on a couple of swings and see what results it gives you. If it works, congratulations. If it gives you garbage, then your scale factor is likely wrong.

3) Look for harmonic numbers

This is a final verification, but it can also be used to help you select your scale in step 1. I watch a couple different scales on the S&P depending on my time frame, but the one I always liked best on the 5 minute charts was a factor of 12 points per day.

I'm talking about day trading here, so a day consists of more than one bar. If I've got two days shown onscreen, then the price axis will have a vertical range of 24 points (12 points per day * 2 days).

What we can do to check a scale factor is examine the numbers themselves. I've noticed that scale factors tend to be important numbers. So 40 points, but not 38.7888. 40 is a nice, round number, and 38.7888 is not.

If we look at 12 points in the S&P, we find that 12 points times $250 per point is $3000 dollars per day, or $15,000 per week. So the dollar values are also "nice" numbers. We can also look for a relationship to 360, the number of degrees in a circle. 360/12 = 30, also a nice number, and it relates back to the dollar value of $3000. So the numbers work – they are all nice, round numbers.

This last step is not a critical requirement, but it will give you the final thumbs up when a scale is in doubt. If you have a potential scale that is pretty good, but not quite there, you can use this technique to tell you how to fix it. Just look for those round numbers when you relate your scale to the price value of the stock or commodity, as well as to 360.

I mentioned the scale of 12 points per day for the S&P. If you try to use that scale today, you'll find that it's too small and you'll have trouble containing the high and low of the day. This doesn't mean that the scale is broken, only that the volatility of the market has increased. Remember, a good scale remains valid forever. All you have to do to make this work is multiply the scale by a whole number, like 2 or 3, and everything will fall into line.

So instead of using 12 points per day, we can use 12x3 points (36) per day. It's the same base scale, but running at a higher harmonic. This is how markets evolve from scale to scale. When the S&P is going strong and 36 points per day doesn't work, I simply change the multiplier to 4, 5, or even 6. In all cases, I'll have a properly scaled chart and will get useful information out of the vortex.

This is a useful tip to know, especially if you're day trading something like the S&P or e-mini. Longer term stock traders usually don't have to worry about scale multipliers, but it comes in very handy during the day when Alan Greenspan comes on and things get wild and wooly in the pits.

CHAPTER SIX:
Examples

You've just come out of two very technical chapters, so now it's time to take a break and get into some of the good stuff. Below are examples of the Fibonacci Vortex in action:

Example 1:

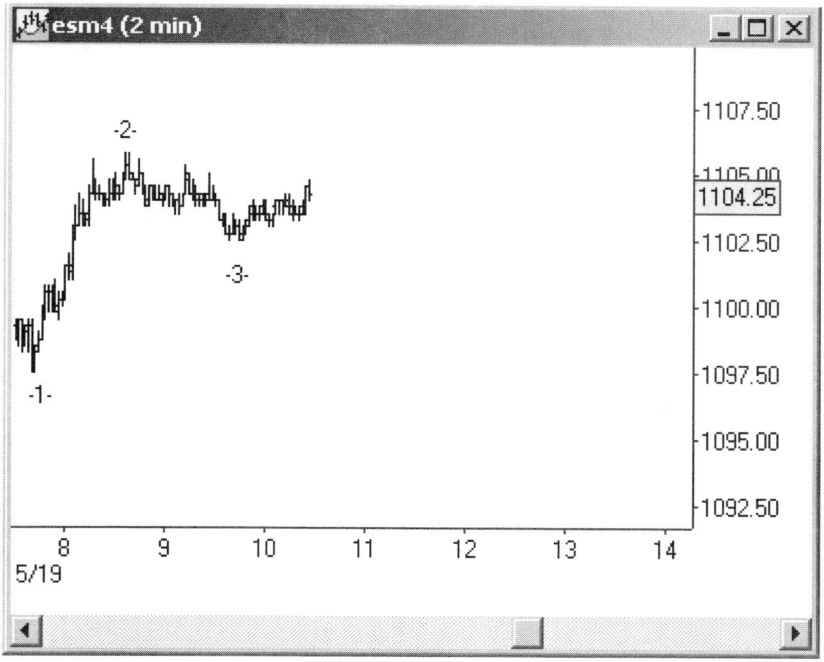

The market has been open for just over two hours, enough time to give us our three swing points. Once we have these three points, we have enough information to place our pattern. Scaling is 0.125 points per bar.

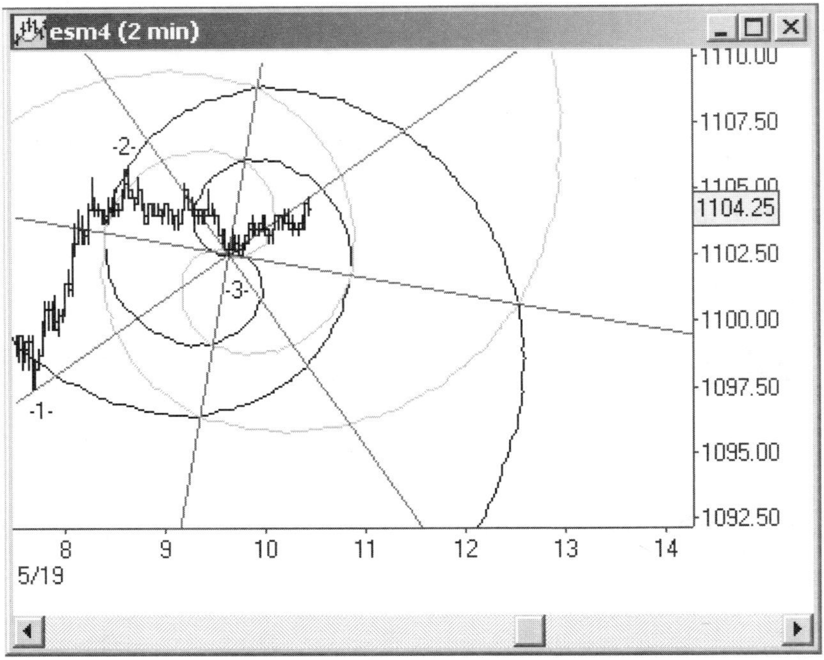

Here's the correct vortex to use. We've got a dark spiral on Point 2, and a spoke on Point 1. We're looking to see where the next high will come in. First resistance is about a half point higher on the dark spiral coming down. But don't forget to check the other vortex:

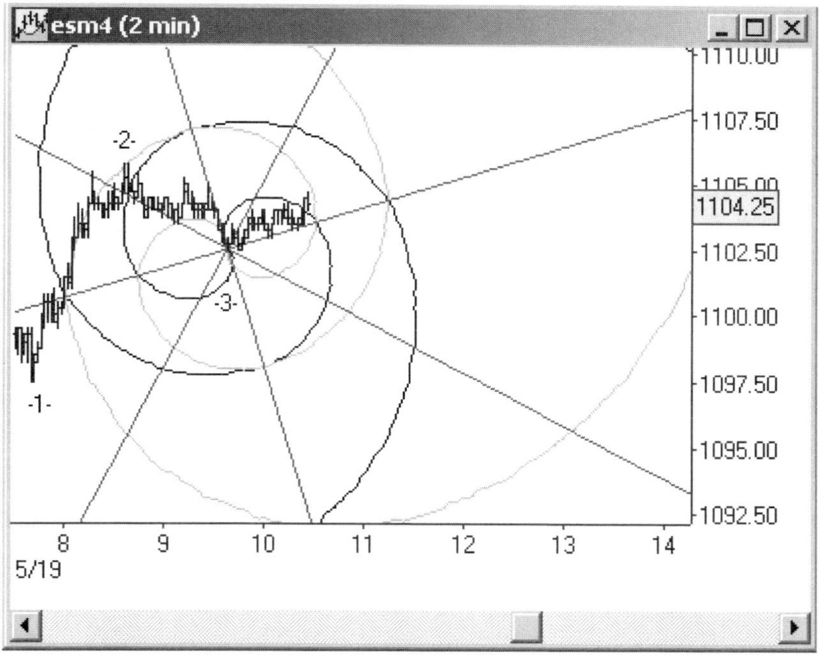

This vortex shows us being right on top of the lighter spiral, so we might experience some resistance here. Note that it's always a lot harder to tell what's going to happen near the center of the vortex, because there are just a lot more lines everywhere. The most reliable signals are the ones based on large swings where price moves to the outer spirals. The inner vortex is a lot more touch and go…

Here's what happened:

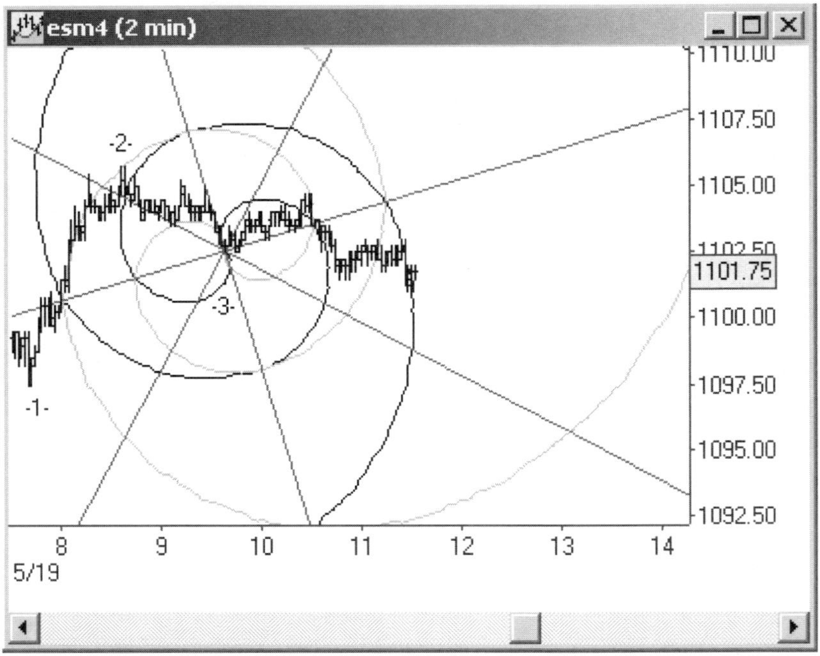

So the lighter spiral was the one after all. Note that the darker spiral did come into effect, but only an hour later after we had already begun to drop. The other thing to notice on this chart is how the rising spoke from the center acted as a great support line, and also provided a sell trigger once broken. These spokes very often create solid trendlines that you can use to help you judge the strength of the spiral signals.

If you look back to the first placement of the vortex in this example, note how price was bouncing up against a spoke right at the high. This is significant when combined with the lighter spiral and the break to the downside of the spoke shown in the chart above. Three spokes and one spiral all working together towards the short side.

Example 2:

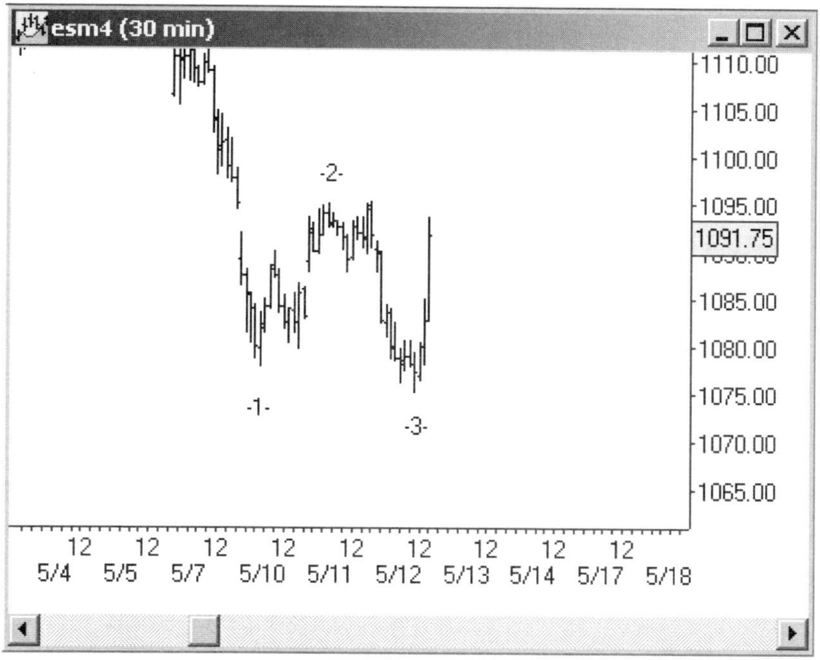

This example is on a 30 minute chart. Scale is 1 point per bar. First step is to select our three points, which I've marked above. That last big bar on the chart is the one that really locks in Point 3, so this is pretty much the earliest we'd have tried to apply the vortex to these points.

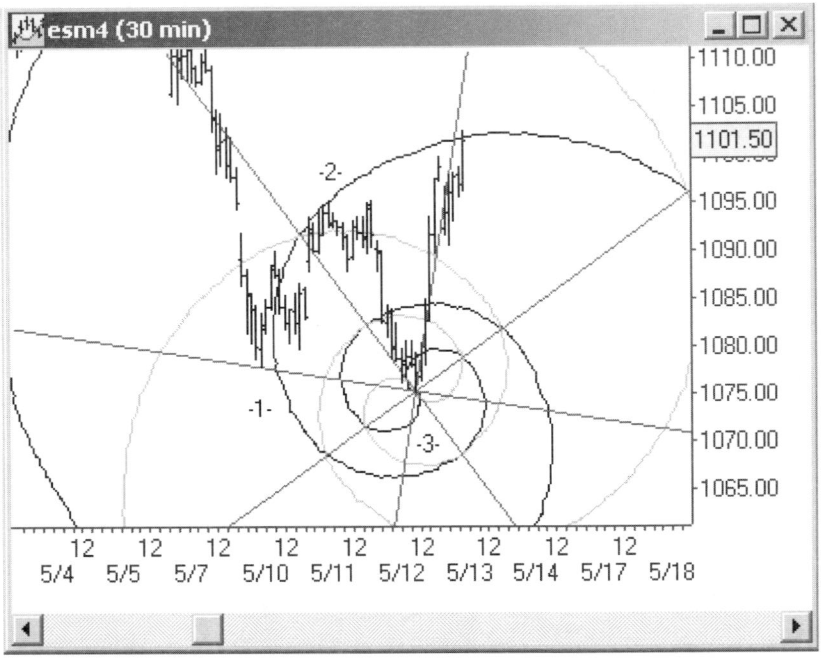

Here's the vortex, shown after a few more bars have taken place. Notice how the spokes are contributing to the pattern match. The sharp impulse wave up that we just experienced ran right along one of our spokes. Now we should see some kind of resistance, as we're running into a dark spiral.

Unlike the previous example, we're out of the crowded inner vortex and have moved into the outer vortex. These are where you'll find the cleanest signals. If we break through the dark spiral, we don't have to pay attention to this vortex again until price reaches the lighter spiral to the outside, which is quite a ways away.

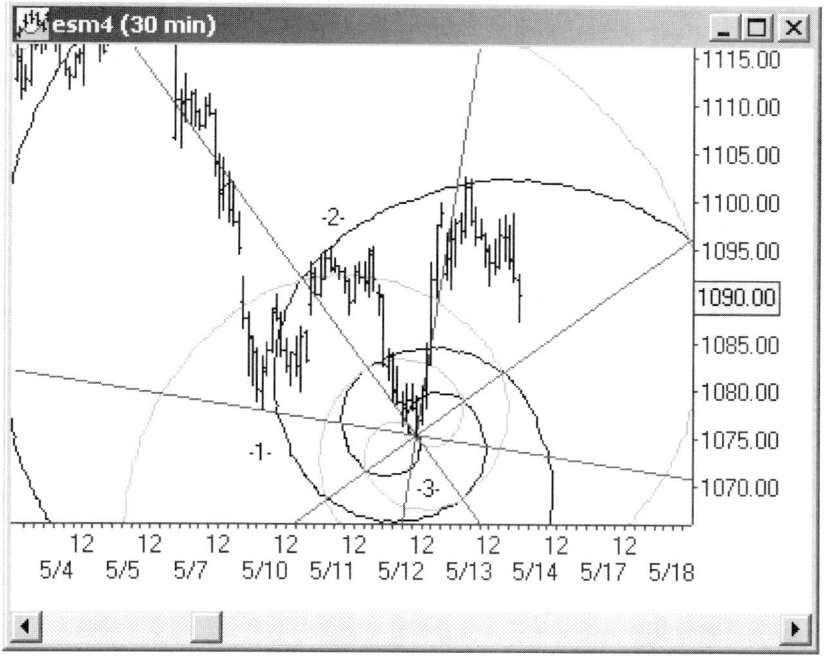

Turns out that we won't have to pay attention to that lighter one after all. Price bounced off the dark spiral as we were expecting. Time to set a new vortex and move to example 3…

Example 3:

Now that price has made another swing point, let's update our labels:

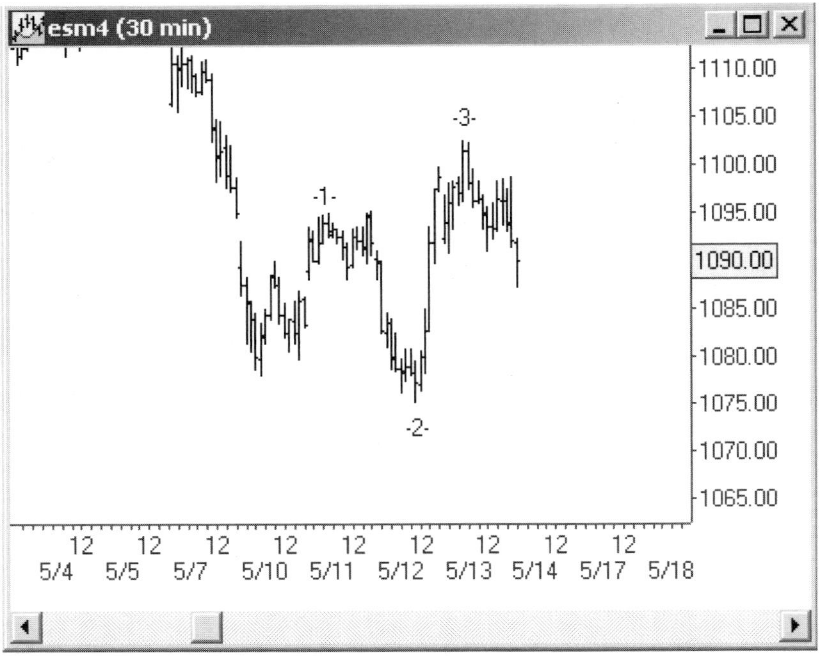

So our latest point becomes the new Point 3, and we go through the familiar process of matching spirals and spokes. Here's the result:

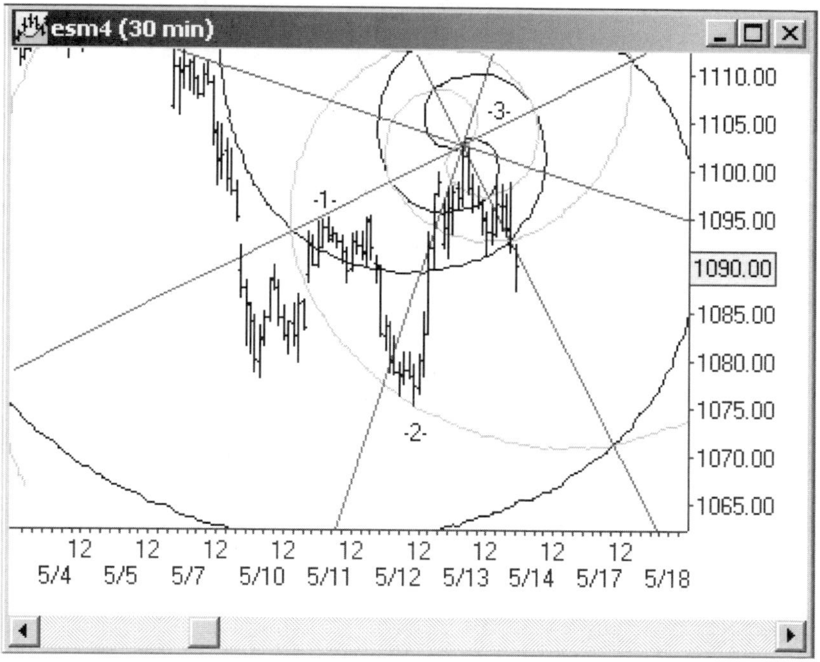

Our first support level is all the way down at around 1070.50 where the light spiral is sitting. We won't have to worry about that one for awhile, so let's rotate to our second vortex and see what it has to say.

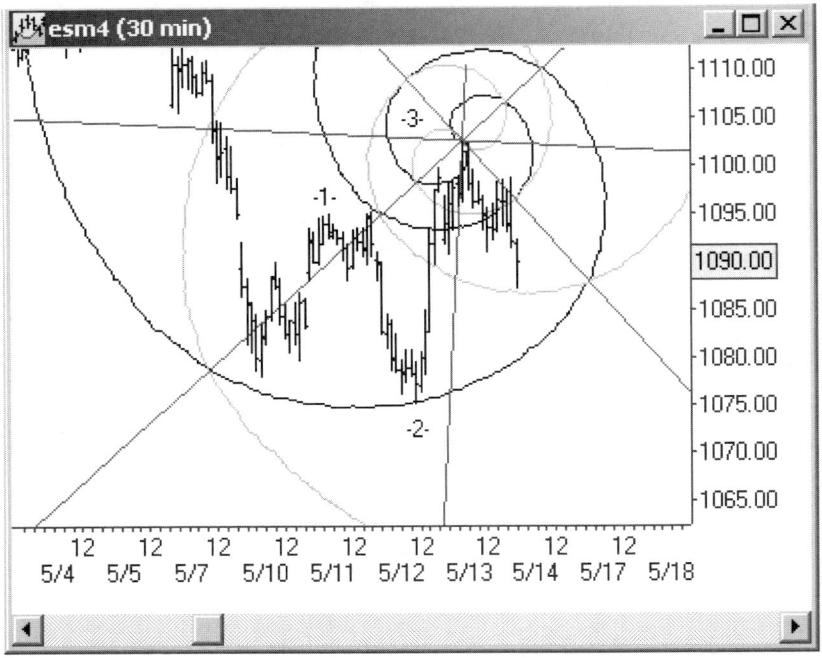

Now we have some spirals to work with. The market is right on top of a light one now, so we might see a bounce here. Alternatively, if we break through this low we need to pay attention for a bottom on the dark spiral a few points underneath.

Let's fast forward a bit more…

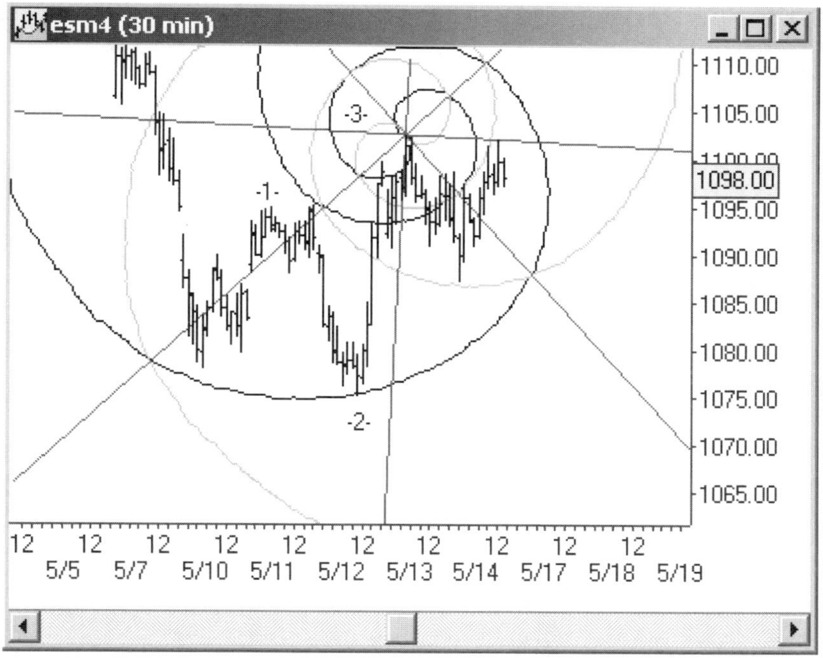

Price did bounce off that light spiral, and it's run up all the way to our spoke, which seems to be containing the rally. So was that the low? Should we set another vortex and look for a top? That would be one option. But these last two waves that we have seen are half the size of the ones that we used to size our vortex. This tells me that it might be a price swing of lesser degree than the ones we're trading, so it might be too early to place a new vortex.

The key factor here is to watch if our spoke at the current high holds. If price can break through that, and take out Point 3, then it's time to set a new vortex for sure. If not, we can keep this one. We have to watch closely over the next few bars to see what course of action we need to take…

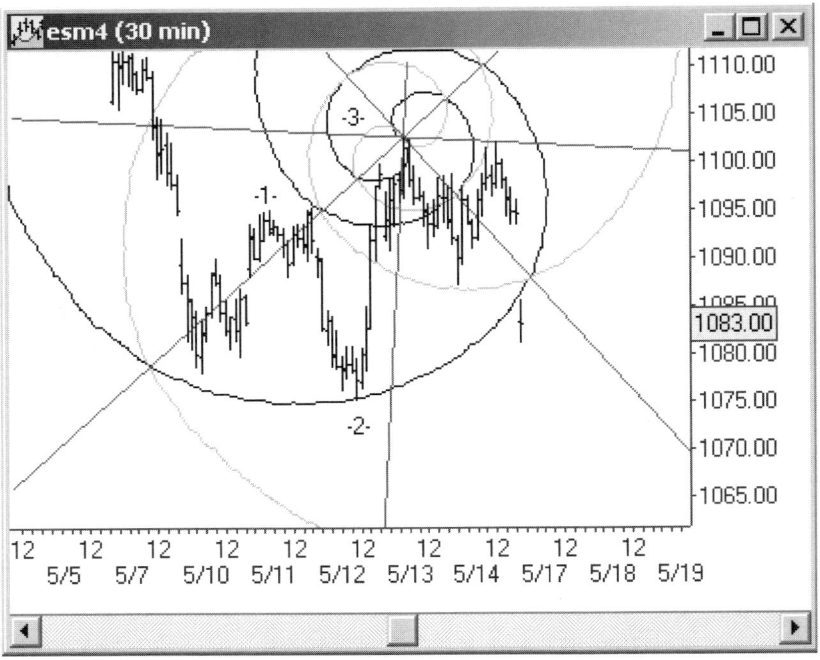

Whoa! The spoke held, but price gapped through our support levels. This vortex looks like it's all used up. There aren't any more spirals to work with here. So it's time to go back to our original:

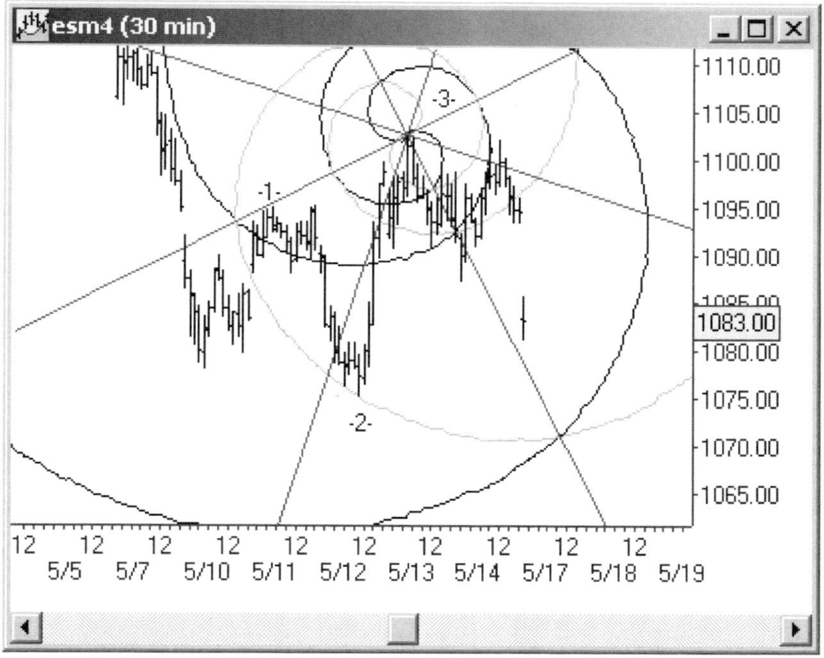

We've still got a ways to drop before we encounter any spirals. But looking ahead, I really like the look of that nodal point at around 1071 where the light and dark spirals intersect…

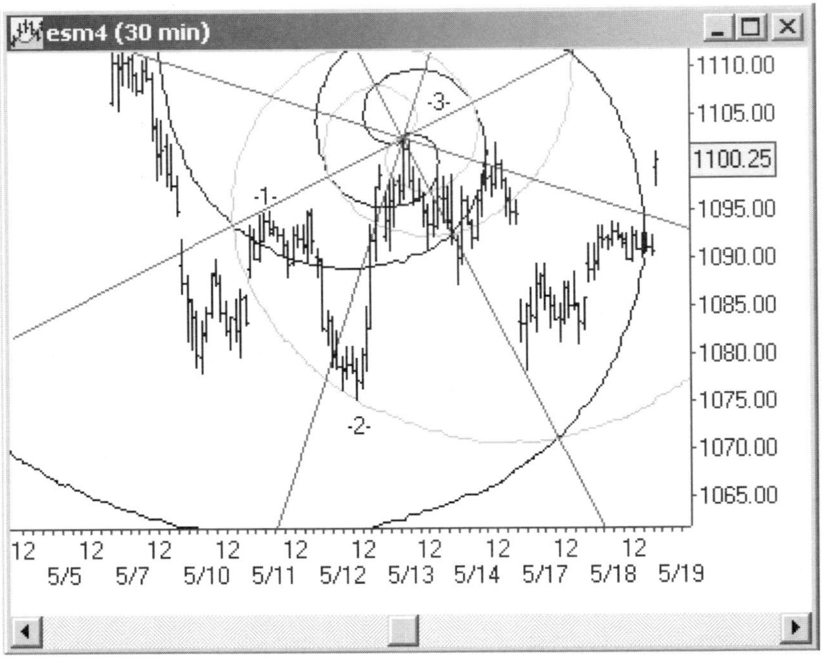

But it was not meant to be. We never got down to our nodal point, and with the big move up it's definitely time to be looking at a new vortex pair.

So did this vortex fail to catch the low? Not really. Take a look at the spoke at the low. That's pretty exact. Spokes aren't usually strong enough to do that, but this one was. It's good to throw an example of this in here, because you need to be aware that this can happen. Got to watch those spokes!

Example 4:

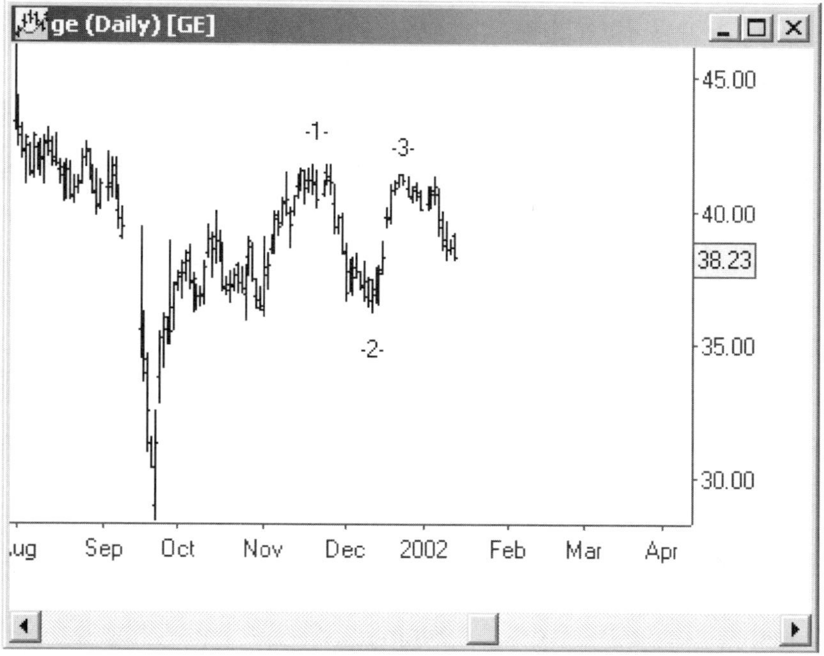

This is a daily chart of GE, scaled to 3 points per month. After the crazy spike low due to September 11th, the market has returned to a nice swinging pattern, and has formed three clear swing points, which of course compels all vortex traders to action:

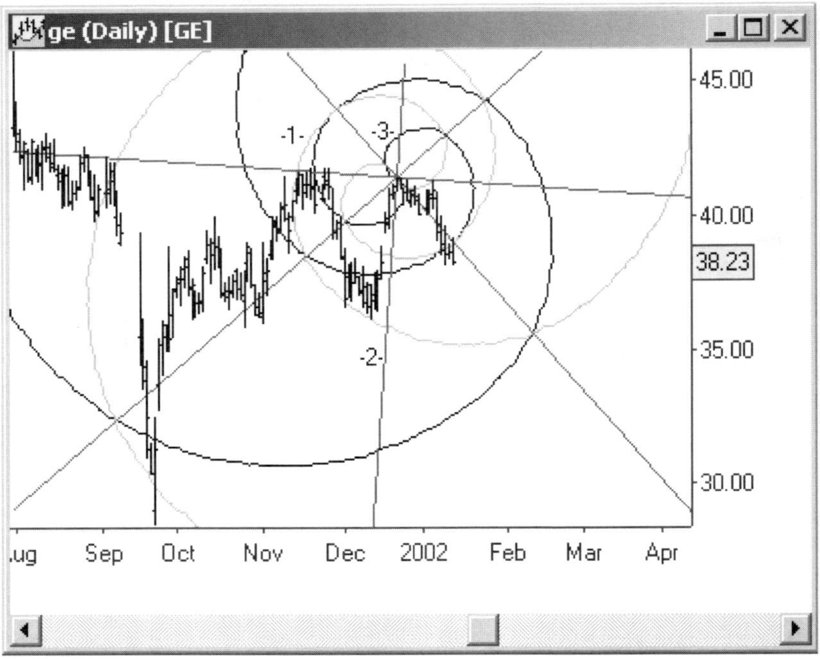

Looking ahead, this vortex placement suggests a decline into a price of around 35, represented by the light spiral below us. We also need to take a look at the second vortex, given by the dark spiral through Point 2:

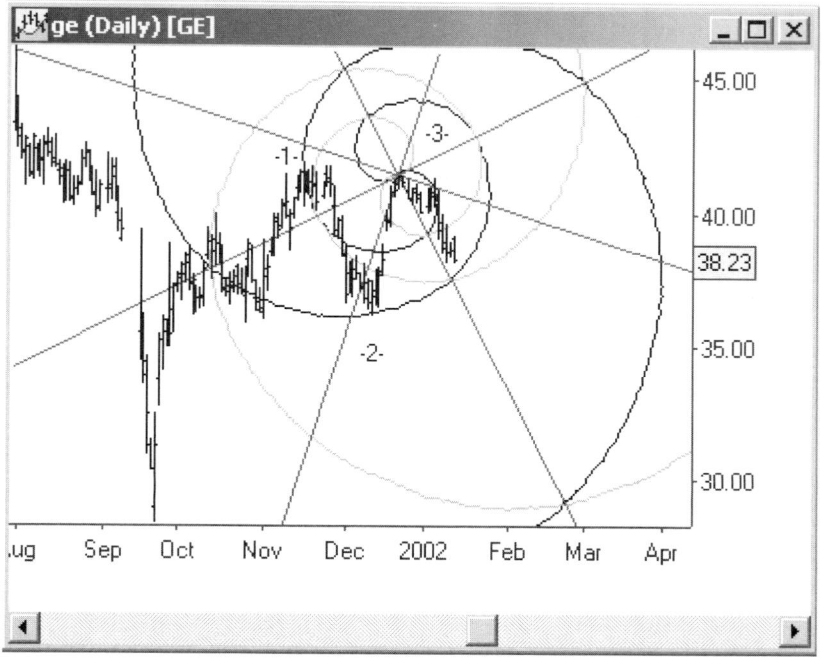

This vortex shows us approaching a spiral cluster now, which creates another possibility of a bounce right away. So we have two possibilities. Either we make a low in the next few days, or we break through the spirals at 38 and head down into 35. If you wanted it both ways, you put in a buy limit a point or so lower, and a stop and reverse below the spirals. But if you think the current swing is just too small to count, then you wait for the break, sell it, and hold to 35, which is what happened:

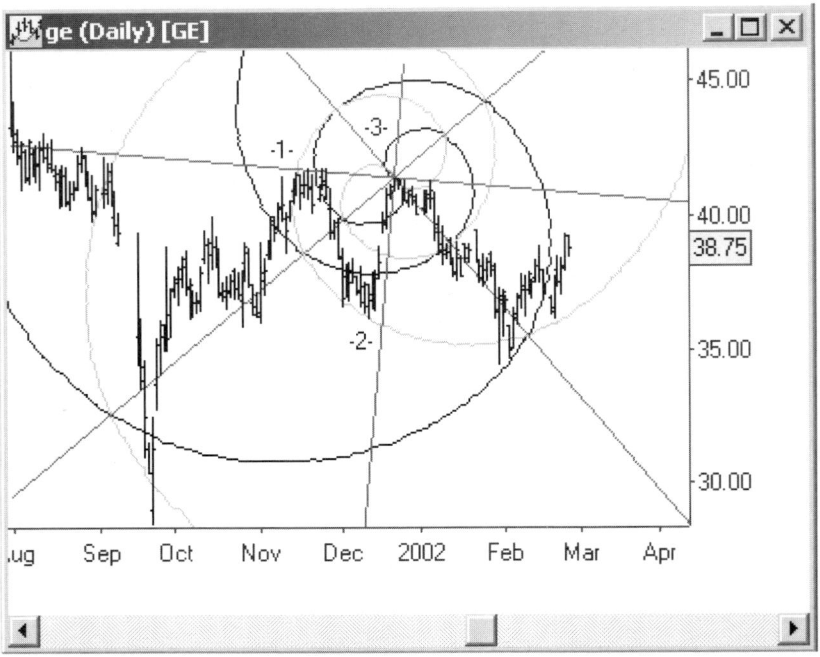

Given that the only support underneath these spirals was way down at 28-29, it was the right time for a bottom and an up swing.

Example 5:

Here's a daily chart of Microsoft, scaled at 10 cents/day.

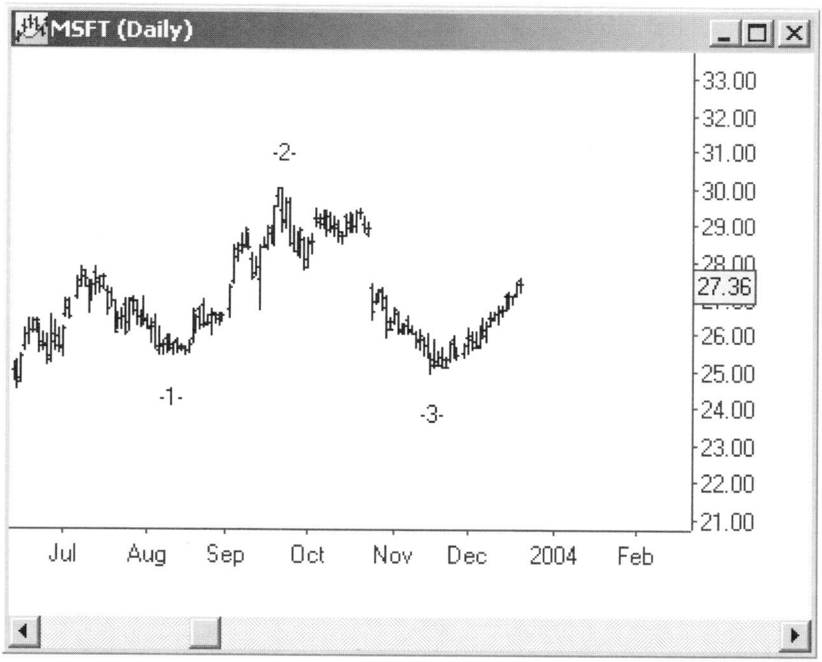

These swings are pretty clear, and we've gone far enough into the current one that we can be confident that Point 3 is for real. Time to place our vortex and take stock of the situation.

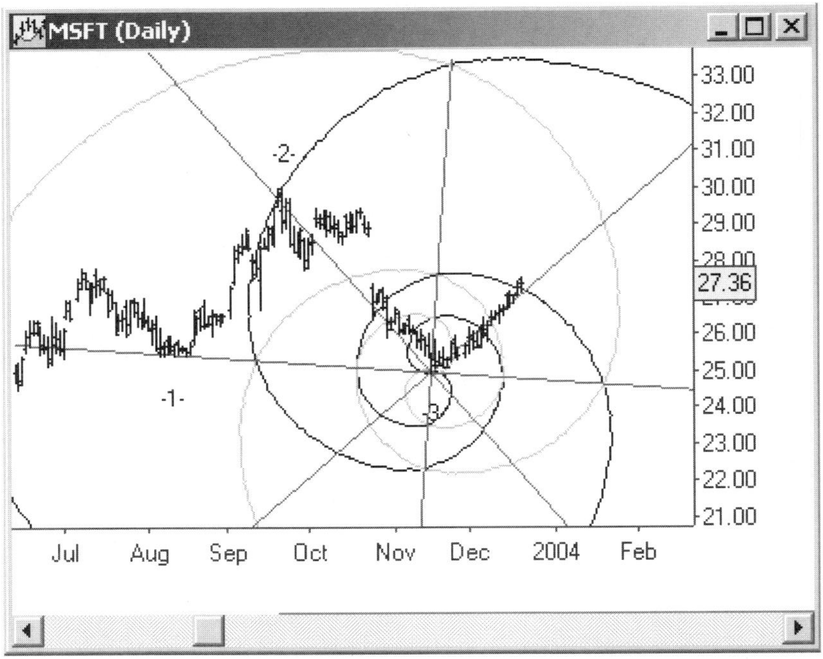

The spokes are very pretty on this chart. We had one running through Point 1, one close to Point 2, and the current upswing is marching very orderly up the third spoke. Now we're at a dark spiral, so there will likely be a pause in the move here. We haven't gone very far in this swing, so this will probably not be the end of it judging by the length of the other swings we've seen. We need to look ahead to the light spiral in front of us. It's hard to get a price on that because it's almost vertical, but time is pretty easy. Looks to be mid-to-late January.

Of course, we still need to check out the other vortex:

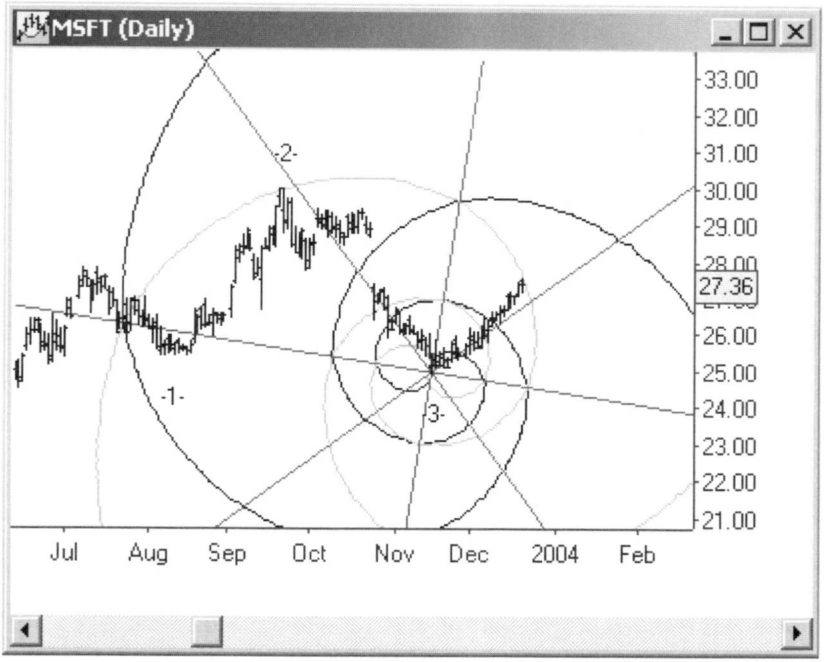

This is interesting. This vortex says we might have a pause here as well. Price is right on the light spiral. If we had a bunch of other things telling us to sell, we could do so here, but I think this swing just got started so it would be a premature short. Look to the outer vortex area for more concrete information.

In this case, the only thing left to work with is that dark spiral. It isn't clear about time, but price is easier to spot than in the last vortex. If we keep on following the spoke the way we are, we'll hit the dark vortex at a price of about 28.50 in late January.

Time to fast forward:

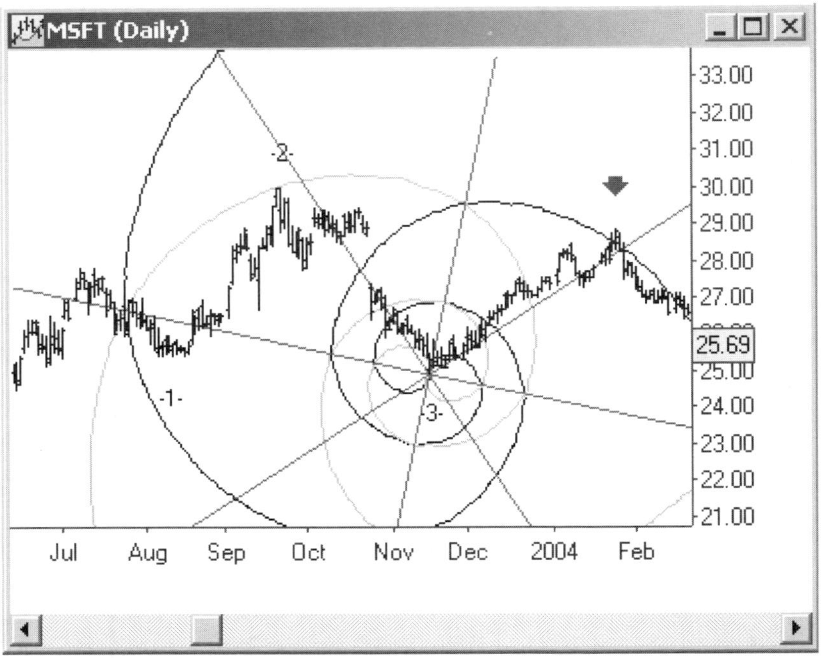

And there's our top! Incidentally, the light spiral was also involved in that top, hitting a bit lower, but within 3 days of the actual high. Price then went on to take out the low at Point 3.

So we've gone over 5 examples of the Fibonacci Vortex in action, which should have cleared up many doubts about how to use this tool to analyze markets. And as 5 is a number in the Fibonacci sequence that governs the growth of all things, that means this must be the last example for this chapter. Time to move on, and take a look at vortex time targets…

CHAPTER SEVEN:
Vortex Time Targets

There is a technique that we can use to get specific time targets from our vortex pattern. It is a little different than what we've been doing up until this point, and is best understood if you think of the vortex as an energy pattern rather than a drawing on the chart.

Imagine that each spiral is not a line, but a collection of points arranged in a spiral pattern. Further, imagine that each point is like a small energy center, radiating outward with a specific force.

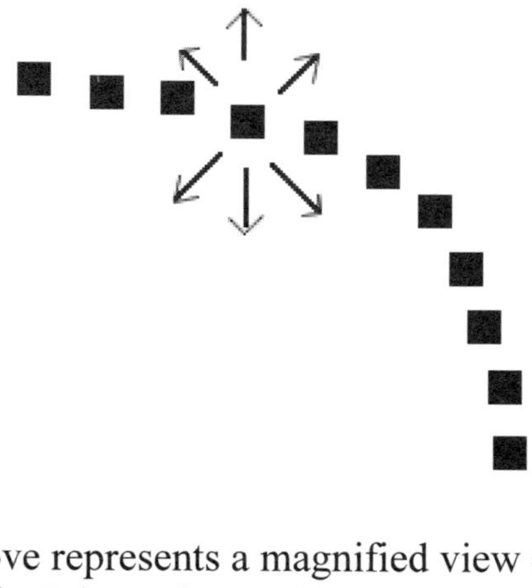

The graphic above represents a magnified view of a section of one of our spirals. It is made up of individual points, each of which has some energy that it is radiating outward.

Taken individually, this energy doesn't amount to much. It's just a single point among thousands of other points. But something interesting happens when we take a look at a group of these points all working together.

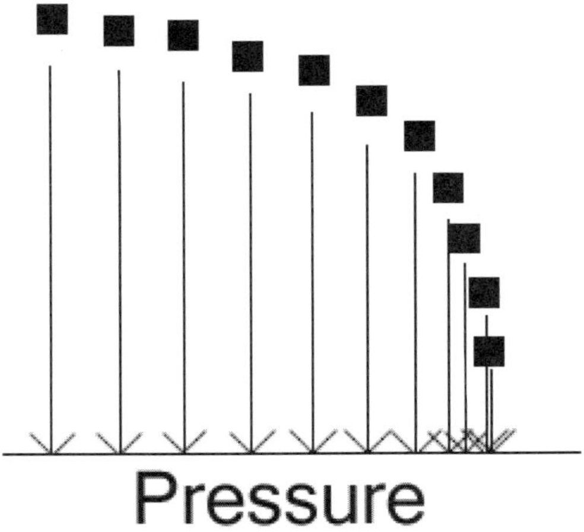

Imagine we are the time axis at the bottom of the chart, looking up at a spiral above us, and measuring the force we feel from each point. When the spiral is going horizontal, like at the top, we find that each point contributes a bit of pressure, but at evenly spaced intervals. However, once the spiral starts going vertically, the points start stacking up on each other, creating a combined force at one spot. The maximum force would be felt when the spiral went totally vertical, and the minimum force would be felt when it was totally horizontal.

Now, keeping this idea in mind, let's take a look at a chart:

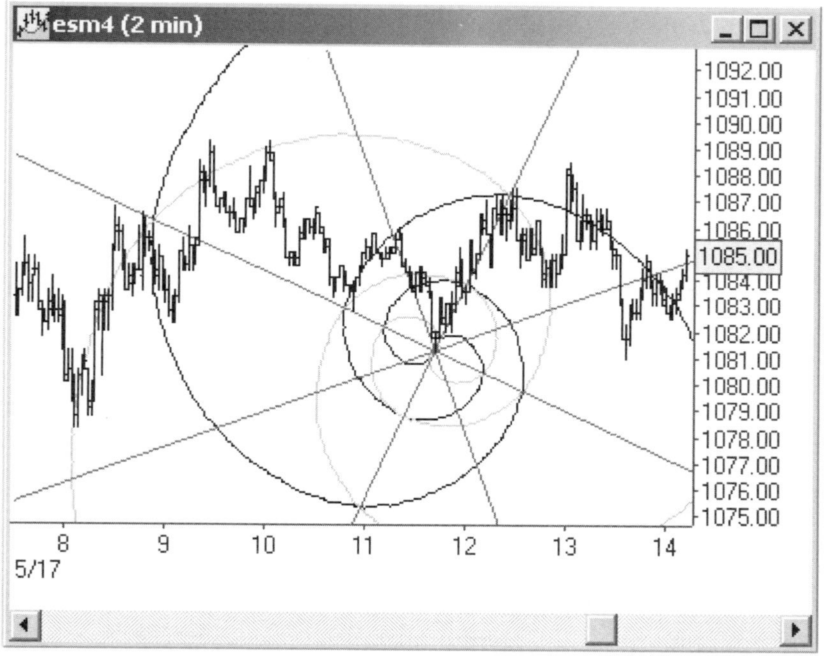

I've placed a vortex at the low in the middle of this day. If we do the same experiment here as we did on the previous page, we can use the vertical sections of the vortex to locate pressure points along the time axis.

Let's draw some lines to make this clear:

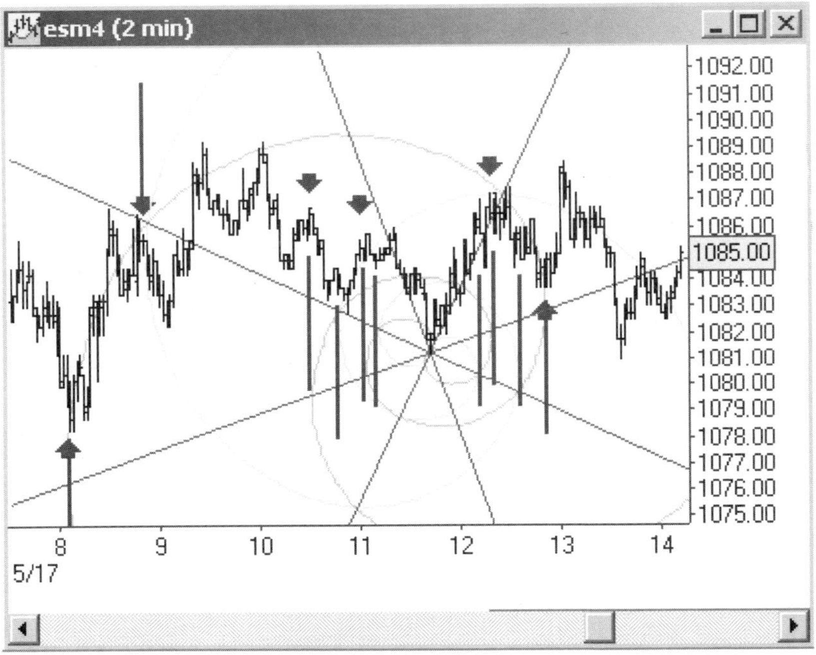

I've put in thick lines in at all the spots where we had a spiral go vertical. You can see that price reacted at every single one of these locations. It wasn't always a major reaction – sometimes it was just a wiggle on the chart – but there was always *something* there. The arrows are there to mark off a few of the ones that jumped out at me.

So what this means is that these vortex patterns are working in more than just one way. We get our spirals and spokes on the chart that give us our major indications, but we also get an entire set of time targets based on spirals going vertical.

We can use these time targets as a way to confirm our vortex signals. Let's take a look at how this can be done:

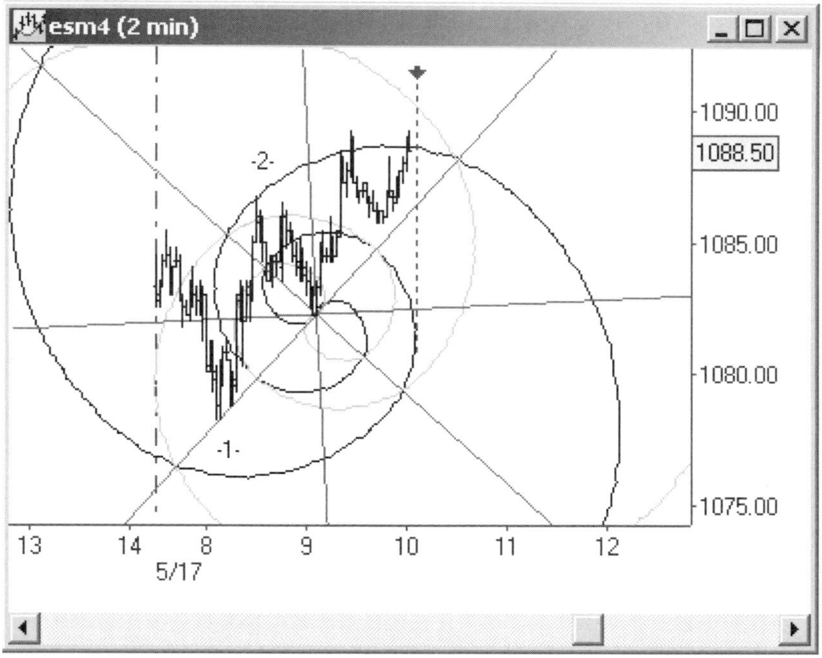

This is a 2 minute E-mini chart, scaled at 0.125 points/bar. I've set the vortex up to project a high, and the market is currently testing the dark spiral. Note that at the same time, we're closing in on a time target, drawn from where the dark spiral goes vertical around 10:00. So we've got our regular resistance signal with price pushing up against the dark spiral, and we've also got a time target due to hit in one bar.

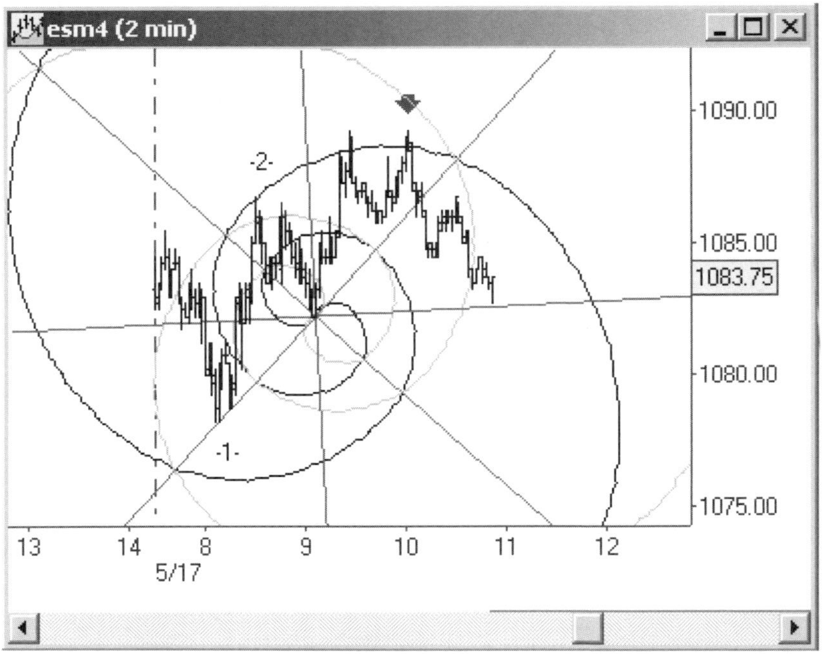

As you can see from the chart above, these two signals combined to drop the market back down to the level of the center of the vortex. One interesting thing to note is that the market tested the dark spiral at the high two different times, and only broke after we had a spiral and time target come together at the same time.

Another useful thing to notice is that these time targets extend into the past as well. This gives us a very easy way to confirm whether or not we are using a vortex that the market will respect. All we have to do is look back in time and judge whether or not the time targets have been accurate.

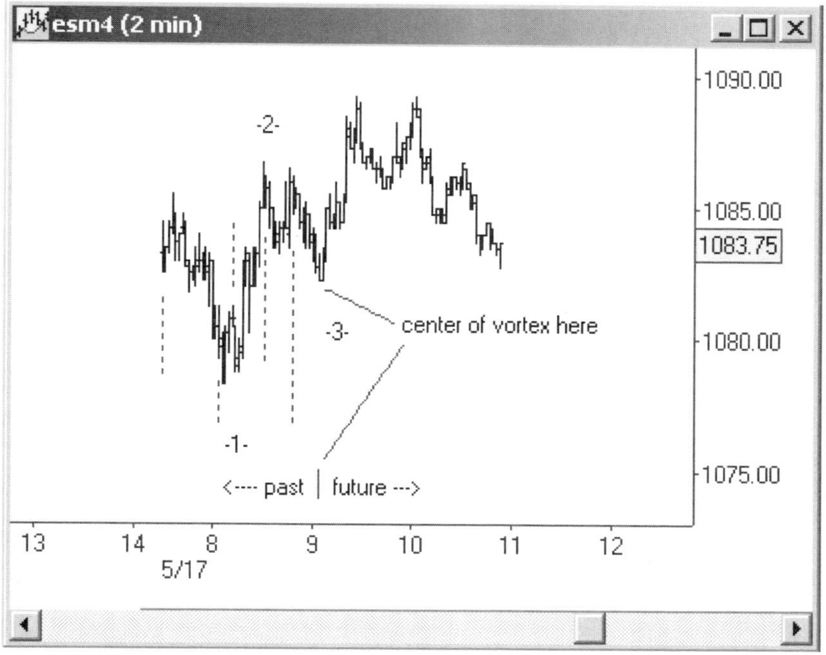

In the chart above, I've drawn in dotted lines from the vortex we just used. These lines came from when spirals (from both vortexes in the pair) went vertical before Point 3. You can see that there is a high correlation between these points and the price action, as tops and bottoms are picked off very closely.

Because of this, we can be very confident that the swing points we are using are correct, and that the market will respect the vortex based on these swings. If we didn't see any correlation between past time targets and our vortex, then we would have a strong indication to be very cautious in our forecasting. It doesn't mean that our vortex wouldn't work, only that there might be other vortexes currently in force that are overriding our vortex. Just as the 15 minute trend can override the 2 minute trend, vortexes based on larger swings can override vortexes based on smaller ones.

Just to make sure everything is clear, let's take a look at one more example:

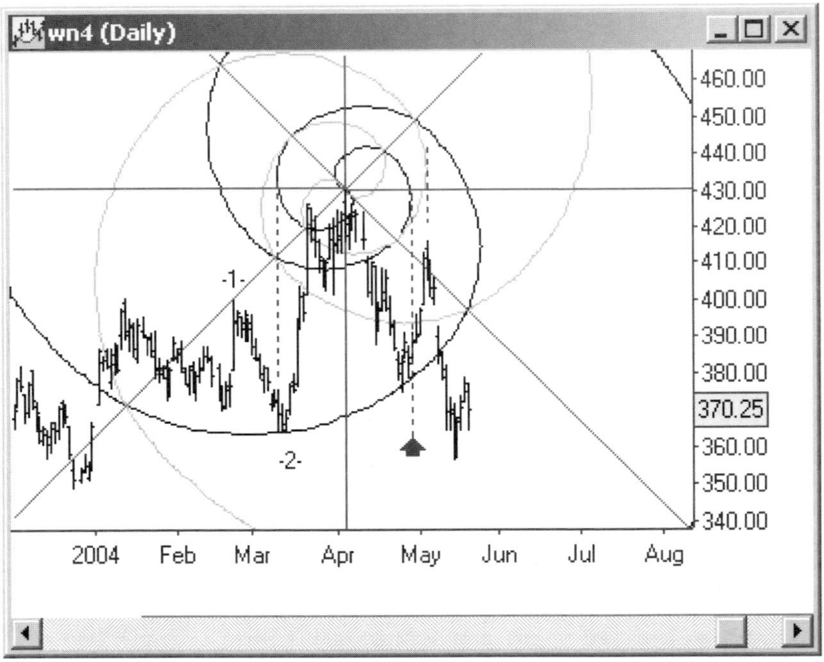

This is a Wheat chart, scaled at 1 point per bar. The vortex was set at the recent high, and the market slid down towards dark spiral, which it hit at the end of April. At this time, we had a time target coming in, and the market found itself bouncing against the vortex at the same time the target was due. This is marked on the chart by the arrow, and we got a nice bounce back up into our next time target from the lighter spiral, which stopped the rally and continued the downward trend.

If you look back in time, you'll notice that Point 2 was accompanied by a time target, also from the dark spiral. A time target at this important low helps us to confirm that we are indeed using the correct vortex, and that we can trust it as the market moves forward.

So time targets can be a very important part of your analysis when you apply the vortex to price charts. You can't trade them totally on their own, but they can work marvelously when combined with spirals and spokes.

CHAPTER EIGHT:
Vortex Price Targets

If you were paying attention during the last chapter, this one will be a piece of cake. By changing our perspective from the time axis to the price axis, and going through the same exercise about splitting the spirals into points, we arrive at the following diagram:

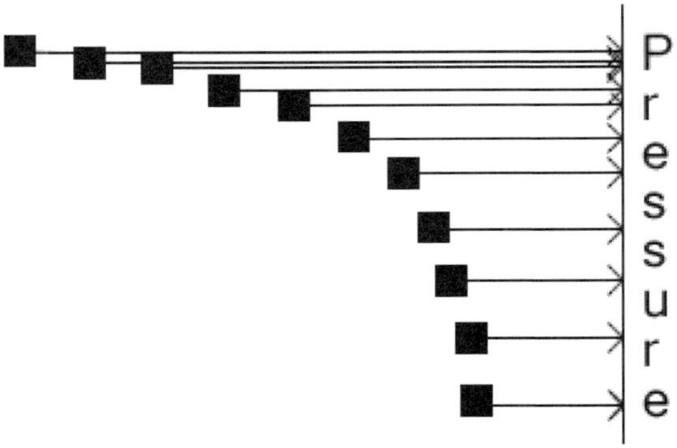

In this case, we have more hits along the price axis when our points go horizontal, and fewer hits when the points go vertical. We saw in the last chapter that spirals going vertical produced time targets. Similarly, we should be able to get price targets by noting when the spirals go horizontal.

Let's take a look at a chart:

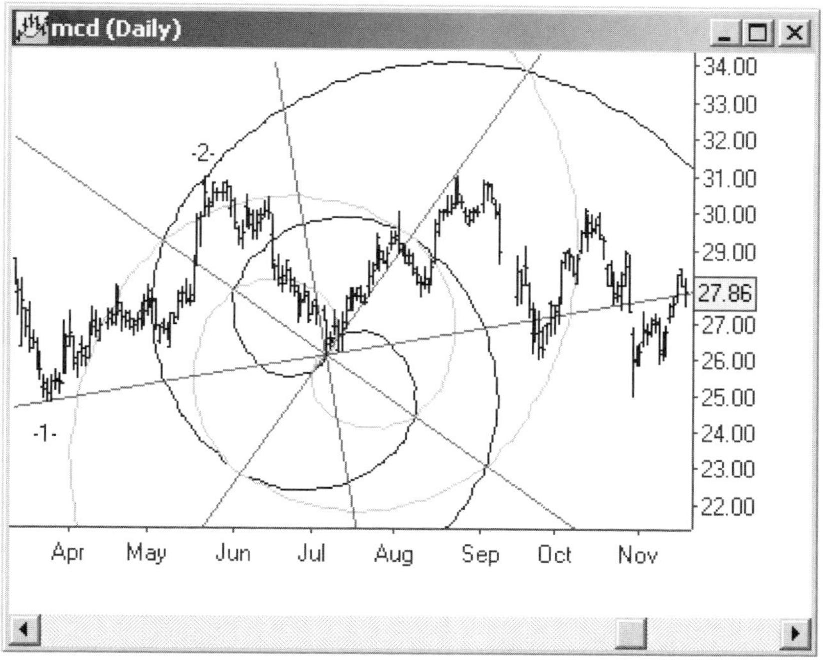

This is a daily chart of MCD, scaled at 0.1 points per bar. I've placed a vortex based on the points as marked on the chart. If you take a look at the price levels where the vortex spirals went horizontal. you'll see that they mark a number of important support and resistance levels, both to the right and left of the center of our pattern.

I'll draw these on the chart to make this perfectly clear:

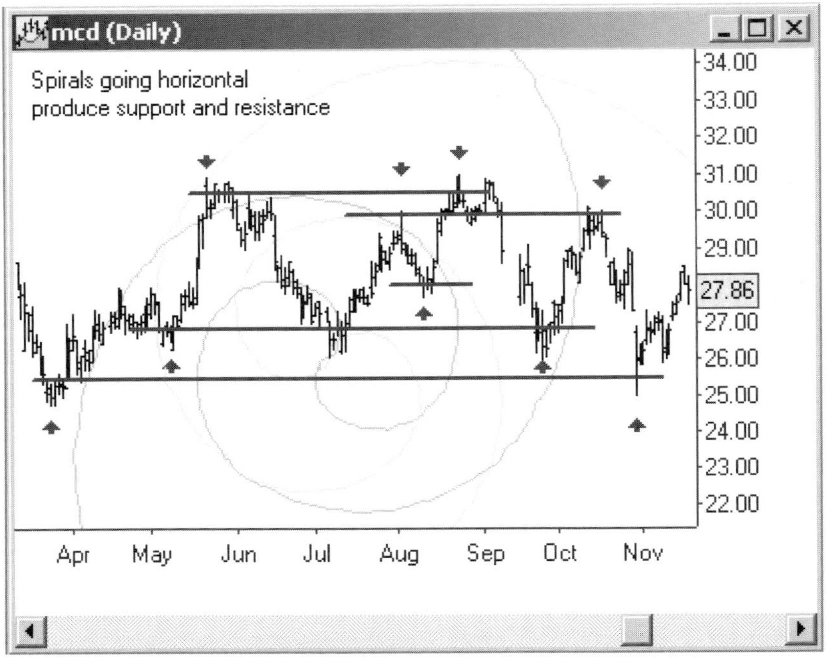

You can see that when considered in the light of price targets, this one vortex was responsible for every single support and resistance level on the chart.

These price targets should be used in the same way as we used the time targets. They are primarily a confirmation tool for our spirals, but they can also give us a hint as to whether or not our vortex pattern is placed properly. Remember, these targets extend both to the future and to the past, so as we are placing the vortex we should be able to look to the recent history of the chart for verification of our price levels.

It's a strange thing to thing to think that the market is reacting to the price levels of a vortex pattern even before the vortex pattern has been placed. We require three points to place the vortex, yet these price and time targets show up even before the first point is completed on the chart. If you believe that markets are random and turning points just happen to fall where they may, it becomes very difficult to wrap this phenomenon around your brain. It just seems impossible that the market could be respecting a tool that will be placed months and even years into the future. It's analogous to complaining about a stomach ache you have now from something you are going to eat in a week or two. Seems as though the cause and effect are going the wrong direction in time!

However, if you believe markets are based on geometric progression and have an inherent natural form, then this is really no big deal. We can give school children one quarter of a circle and they can easily sketch the missing area because they how to construct a circle. They know how it's all supposed to look and can extrapolate. Similarly, the market knows exactly where it's going and how it is supposed to look. Just because a turning point hasn't formed on our charts doesn't mean that it's not there. It's just that the market hasn't gotten around to building that turning point yet. But it will all happen in due course. We personally might not know about the important high that's going to appear in a year, but the market does. Each day is not an independent event, separate from all other days, but a connected series of elements in a complete, unified pattern. Each day has it's place, and a specific geometric relationship to all past and future days. And that's how you can see these patterns having an effect reaching both into the future as well as into the past.

So let's take a look at an example now, and see how these price levels can help us confirm vortex signals:

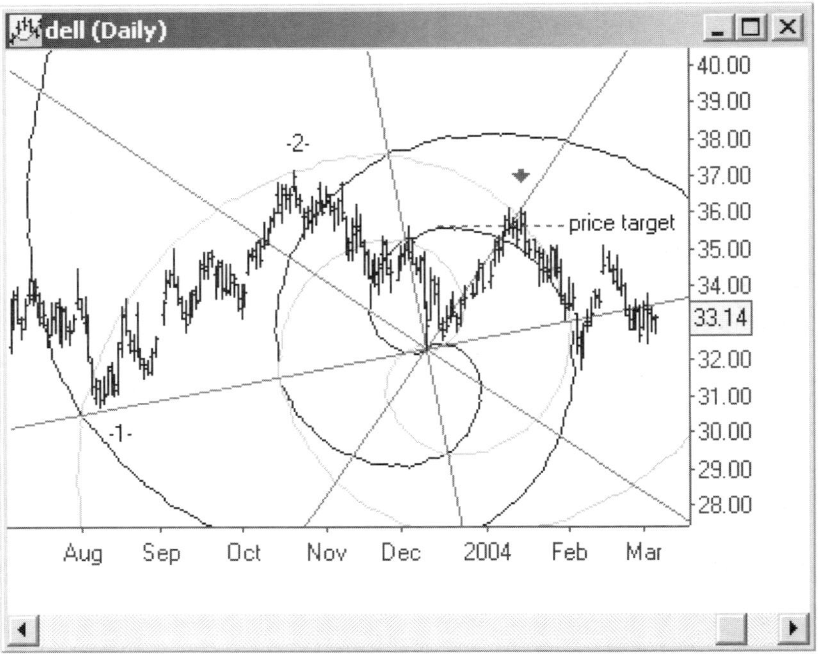

This is a daily Dell chart, scaled at 0.1 points per bar. The market has rallied from the center of our pattern along a spoke until it ran into the light spiral arching down from the high at Point 2. Note that this was also the location of a price target derived from a dark spiral going horizontal.

When the market hit the intersection of the spiral and price target, it was time to drop, and you can see that it followed the light spiral down to below vortex center, where it finally was able to break free.

There is actually a lot more going on in this chart than just that, and we'll be coming back to it in the next chapter.

CHAPTER NINE:
Time and Price Squares

So now you have three timing techniques that you can use based on the Fibonacci Vortex. The first is watching as price bounces off the light or dark spirals, the second is to track time targets based on spirals going vertical, and the third is to track price targets based on spirals going horizontal. Now it's time to put them all together.

Each of the techniques works well on it's own, but when you combine them, you get a truly powerful set of tools to locate turning points in the market. The method I use is to put primary emphasis on the spirals, and use the time and price targets to confirm them. This keeps everything simple, and the targets provide a quick and easy way to gauge the strength of a particular spiral.

I have noticed that the strongest patterns occur when all signals are based on the same color spiral. So if price is bumping up against a dark spiral, what I'd really like to see is a time/price target confirming that which is also based on a dark spiral. They can be from different vortexes in the vortex pair, but the colors should be the same. Having said that, I've seen plenty of trades where the colors were mixed, but they don't seem to be quite as exact as the ones where everything is the same.

In the last example from the previous chart, we caught a swing high in Dell using a vortex and price target. Let's return to that chart, because there is a lot more here to study:

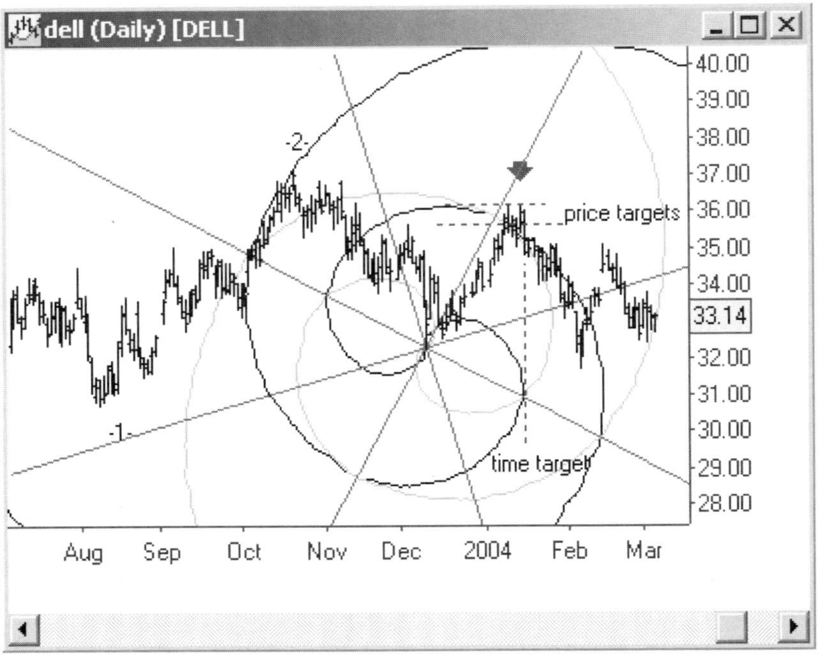

This time, we've got the other vortex working. I've left in the price target from before, and this vortex contributes another. Additionally, it contributes a time target. Both the time target and the price target on this vortex come from the dark spirals, and they nailed the high about as exactly as you're ever going to get. Of course, both light and dark spirals are present at the high as well, plus the one from the other vortex.

So this is what a perfect vortex setup looks like. Multiple time and price targets, multiple spirals, and no slop anywhere to be seen. You don't need much more when you find a setup like this one.

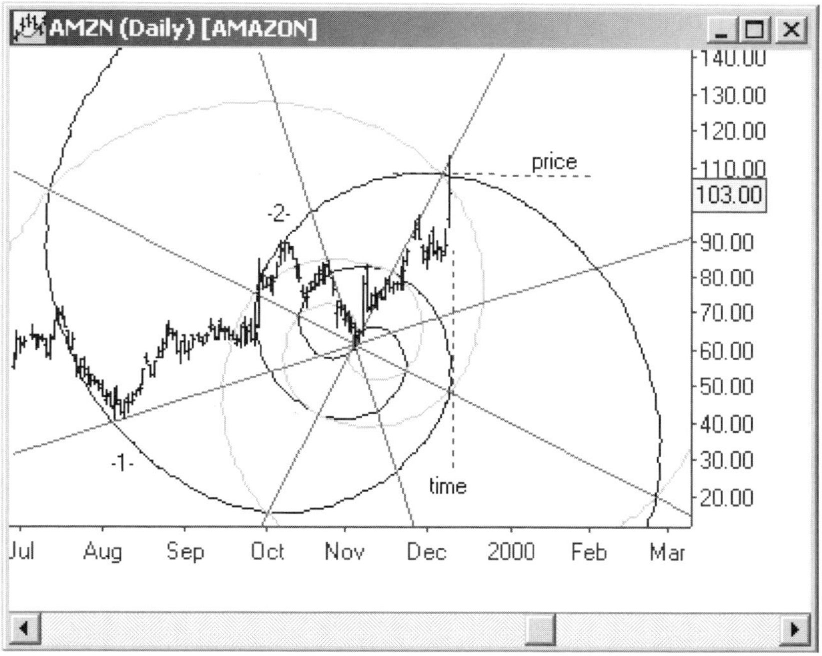

Here's a chart of Amazon, scaled at 1 point per day. On the last bar, price was able to penetrate the dark spiral, but not close above it. In fact, it closed below both the dark spiral and the light spiral, respecting both of these levels. We have a price target from the same dark spiral, and a time target due to hit the very next day, also from a dark spiral. This is a pretty clear setup for a short trade.

Here's what happened:

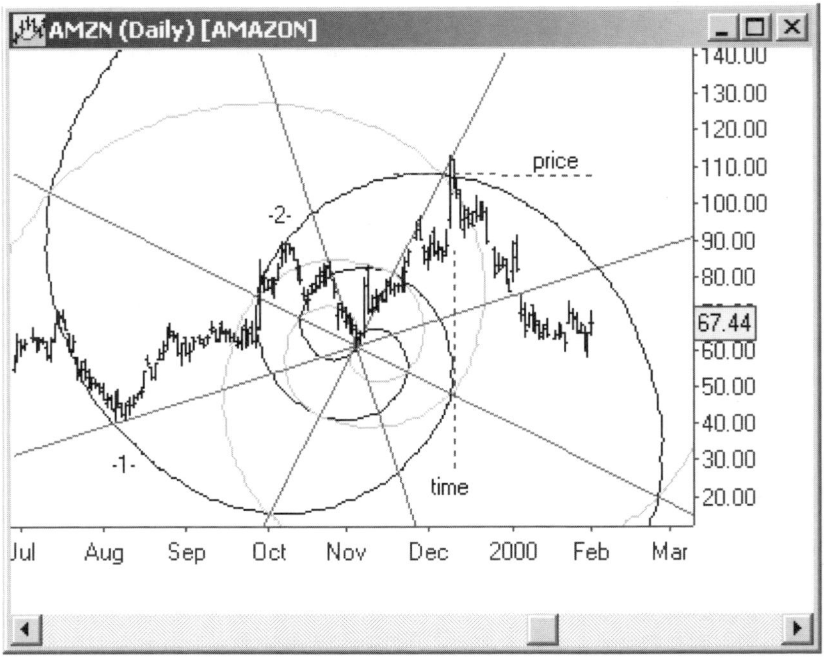

AMZN was unable to get through the thick vortex cluster, and subsequently lost nearly half it's value over the next two months. There were plenty of people who bought this stock there at the top, totally unaware of how the geometry of the market was setting up against them.

This next chart is very interesting:

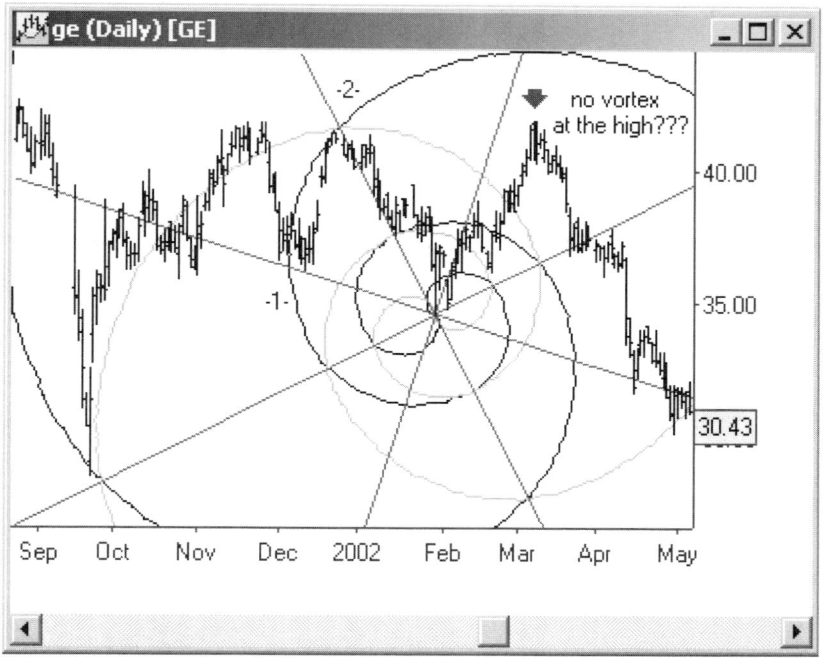

This is a daily GE chart, scaled at 3 points per month. This vortex should be a good one, at least judging by how many of the past time targets nailed previous highs and lows. Those targets are not drawn in on the chart above, but you should be able to pick them out pretty easily now. But despite an exact sizing and confirmation from past targets, we don't have a spiral anywhere near that high at the arrow. The other vortex is nearly identical to this one, as both spirals are very close to Point 2, so it doesn't have a spiral at the arrow either. So what's going on? Did the vortex just crap out on us, or is there something else happening at that high?

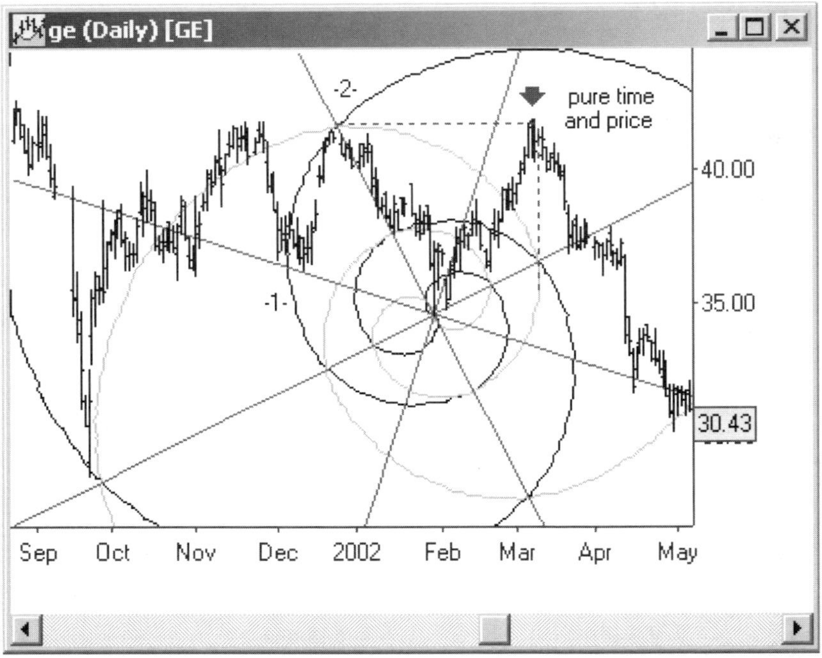

This was a pure time and price top, with both targets being contributed by the light spiral. The intersection between the two was accurate to within one day and 20 cents. If you had been diligently watching your time and price targets, you would have spotted the potential for a top there. But you wouldn't have spotted it if you were just waiting for a spiral hit. This stuff can be a bit tricky, so you've got to stay on your toes!

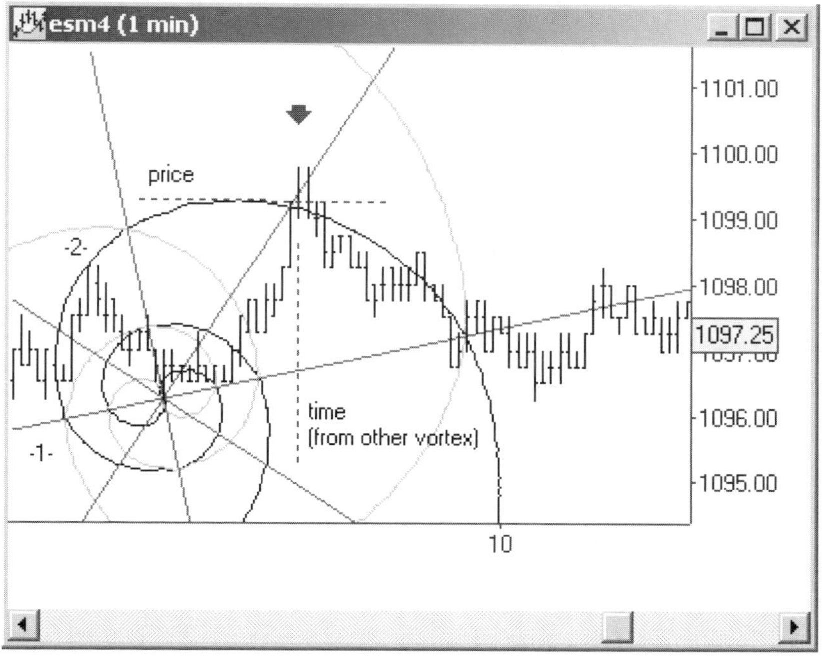

One more example. This is a 1 minute mini S&P chart, scaled at 0.125 points/bar. The time target came from the other vortex, but it was off a dark spiral. The vortex shown provides the price target, and spiral itself. So we had price, time, and spiral all coming together at the high. Note that while price did clear the spiral by two ticks, it was never able to close above the price target. So price and time came together exactly to the bar and within half a point, and it was down from there.

This example happened literally minutes ago on the day I'm writing this. Finding examples for this book is really easy, because it happens like this day after day. There are just so many to choose from. Once you get some practice in applying the vortex, you'll find tons of them in real time that work just like this one did.

CHAPTER TEN:
Integrating the Vortex into Your Trading

Now that you can apply the vortex to a chart to locate high probability reversal areas, there's only one thing left to do, and that's integrate this technique into your trading tool kit.

Those who have read any of my articles know that I constantly harp about using multiple, non-correlated tools to confirm trading setups. The truth is that no one tool correctly explains all market behavior. All tools have conditions when they work well, and conditions when they work not-so-well.

The benefit of using multiple tools together in a unified approach is that we minimize the amount of time that our tools fail us. One tool might go out every now and then, but it will be very rare when the entire tool box crashes on us. That one tool might be screaming for us to sell, but we can filter that signal by checking our other tools and using them to either confirm or deny the signal from the first.

When you approach trading in this way, you'll find that a lot of the whipsaw trades tend to disappear. Not only that, you will automatically focus on only the best setups, where you have a predominant number of tools all telling you to do the same thing at the same time. These are the trades that you want to take.

So how you incorporate the vortex into your trading depends on what other tools you are using, and your trading style. If you are a trend trader, you can use the vortex to try and pick the best point to reenter the market after a consolidation period. Alternatively, if you are a short term scalper, you can use it to help you identify the reversal points that you're trying to jump in on.

In any case, you'll find best results if you use it in conjunction with other tools, and not use it as an entire trading system unto itself. The vortex requires judgement to use properly, and as all traders know, your judgement is not a fixed quantity. In the heat of the moment, it's easy to introduce a fudge factor based on fear and greed that will make you think the vortex is saying things that it is really not. When you have your other tools there to cross reference, you'll find that you have a much more objective viewpoint than you would otherwise.

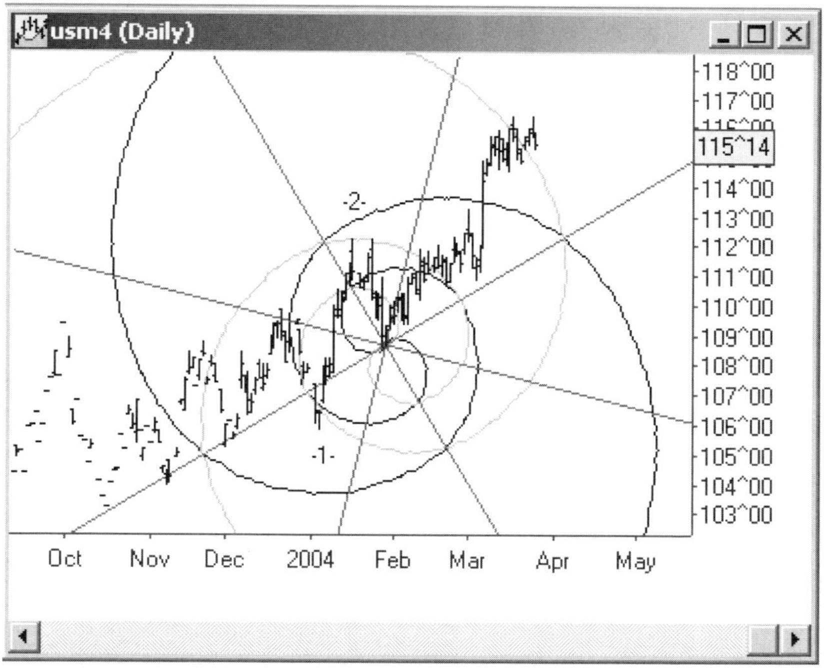

This is a daily Treasury Bond chart, scaled at 0.125 (4 ticks) per bar. You can see that price just ran into the light spiral, which seems to have stopped the rally. However, there are no time or price targets to confirm this signal, so the big question is whether the market will turn down from here, or simply consolidate and then resume the upward trend.

Now is the time to check other tools, and see what they say about this situation.

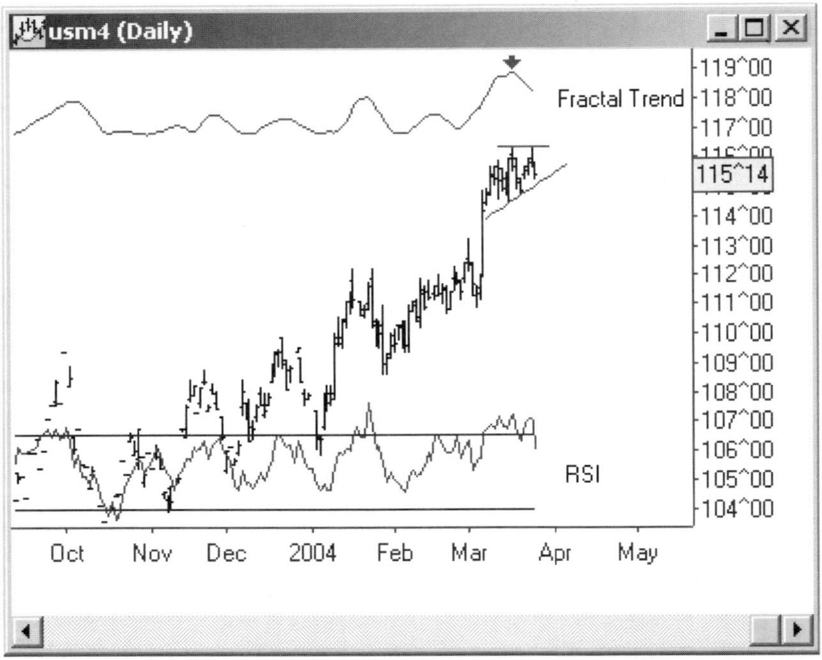

I've added two indicators to the chart above. At the bottom, we have a standard 14 bar RSI indicator. The basic method for using it is to sell the market when the trigger line crosses below the upper threshold, and to buy the market when the trigger line crosses above the lower threshold. This tool has been at oversold levels for about 2 weeks, and has just crossed beneath the upper threshold line. So this classic indicator is telling us to go short, confirming what the vortex alerted us to already.

The indicator at the top of the chart is called the Fractal Trend Index, and is one of the proprietary tools in the Wave59 software package. It works a lot like the ADX, only better. What it does is measure the strength of the trend. So higher values mean the trend is strong, and lower or flat values mean the trend is weak. It recently moved into high territory, forming what looks like the first part of a mountain. This indicates a strong trend. However, note that it just topped out and is beginning to decline. I've marked this spot with an arrow. This means that the force behind the uptrend is weakening, and the market is due for a reversal. This is usually a very reliable indicator when you are looking to pick tops and bottoms, so seeing it top out here like this really gives strength to the vortex.

Finally, the market seems to be making a triangle pattern, giving us some classical technical analysis to work with. If we're looking to sell this market, we can do so on a break of the upward sloping trendline. If price breaks the flat trendline to the upside instead, we'll have to cancel our orders and revise our opinion of this market.

Here's what actually happened:

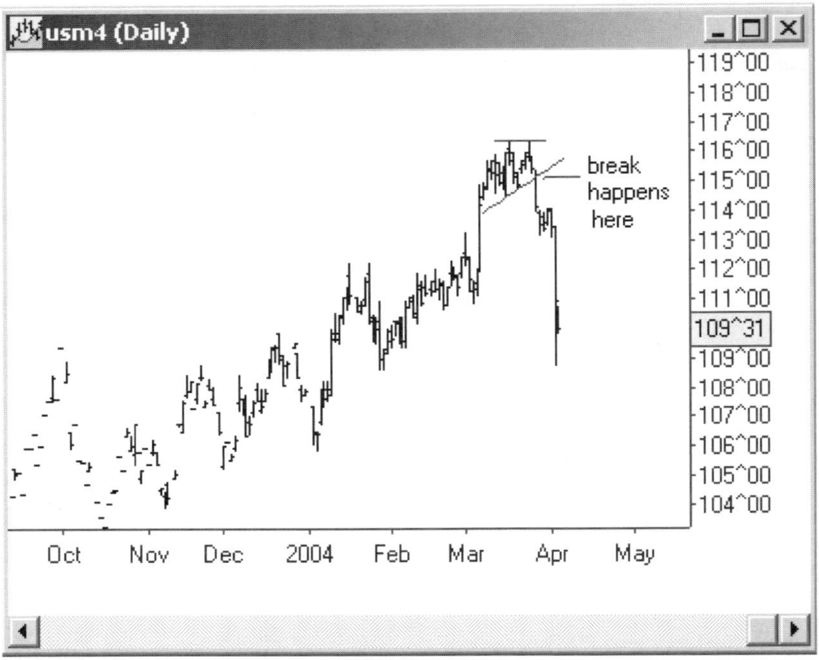

The market did break the upward sloping trendline as expected, and continued down hard. There were some big profits to be made on the short side on this one.

Here's a fun chart:

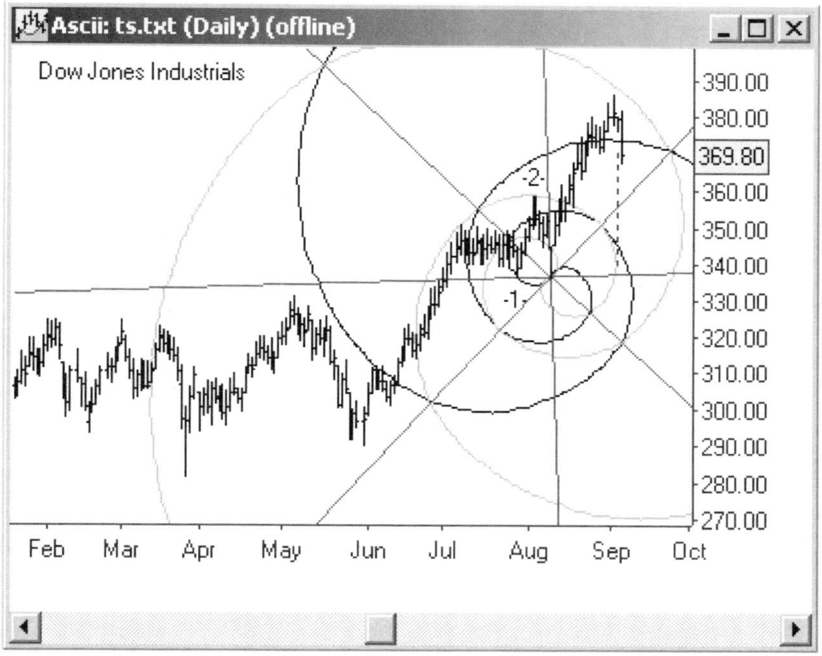

This is a chart of the Dow Jones Industrial Average, back in 1929 before Black Monday. It is scaled at 1 point per bar. It was a little tough finding swing points on this chart, as the consolidation in July was just too flat to really count as a down swing. I finally chose the marked points, which were the only ones that seemed to stand out. The Dow rallied from there just short of the light spiral, and made a top within one day of the time target from a light spiral.

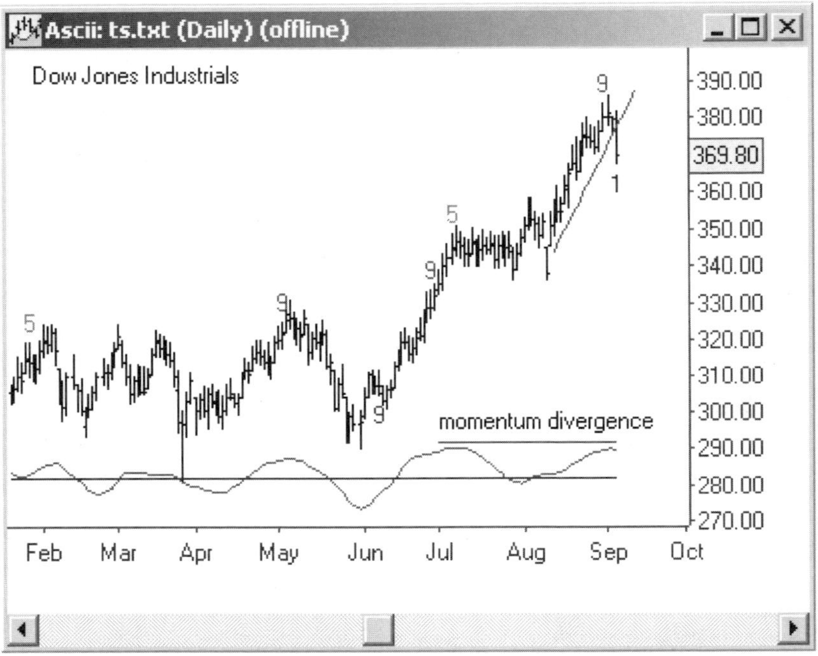

Going back in time to check out crashes is always a fun thing to do, especially when you apply the tools that you are currently using. Two tools that I watch every day are the 9-5 Count and UltraSmooth Momentum curve. These are both proprietary tools that I've put in Wave59.

The 9-5 Count is very simple – just look for 9's and 5's, and turning points should fall near those numbers. You can see how it has been working on the chart above. We had a 9 pop up above price in August, which is a clear indication that this could be a high. So the 9-5 Count agrees with the vortex.

The momentum indicator at the bottom is just like the standard momentum tools that have been around for years, except that it is extremely smooth with very low lag. On the last bar, momentum turned down, confirming a bearish divergence signal that had been setting up for months. This kind of signal occurs when price makes a higher high, but momentum makes a lower or equal high. The indicator and price are said to be diverging in this situation, and 8 times out of 10 price will correct in the direction of momentum. So this is a strong sell signal.

Finally, we've been following a trendline up into the top, and that last bar broke through it strongly. So we have a trigger confirming the short trade as well.

We all know what's going to happen next, but let's check the chart out anyway and see what it looked like:

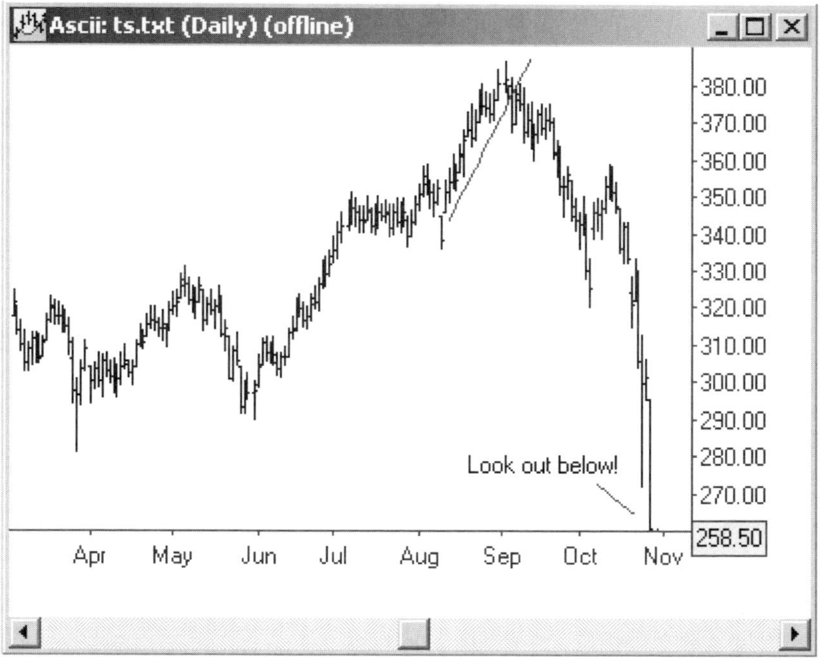

Price has literally fallen off our chart, and the last bar is totally off screen. This happens with scaled charts. They don't stretch, so if things get too wild, you can just go right off the edge. Back in the chapter on scaling, I mentioned multiplying the scale factor by whole numbers like 2 or 3 to take into account volatile periods. This is a time when you'd have to do that. So instead of remaining at 1 point per bar, you'd need to go up to 1x2 or 1x3 instead so that you could get the whole chart on the page.

Hopefully these two examples gave you an idea how to use the vortex together with other tools. It's not a tough thing to do, but it's an important step that will help to keep you on the right side of things and on the correct spiral.

CHAPTER ELEVEN:
Alternative Approaches

In this book, I've shown you what I consider to be the best way to apply the Fibonacci Vortex to price action. This is exactly how I use this pattern when I analyze markets. However, this is not the only method that works, and in this chapter we'll take a look at some alternative approaches that can be used as well.

Method 1: Mixing up the Swing Points

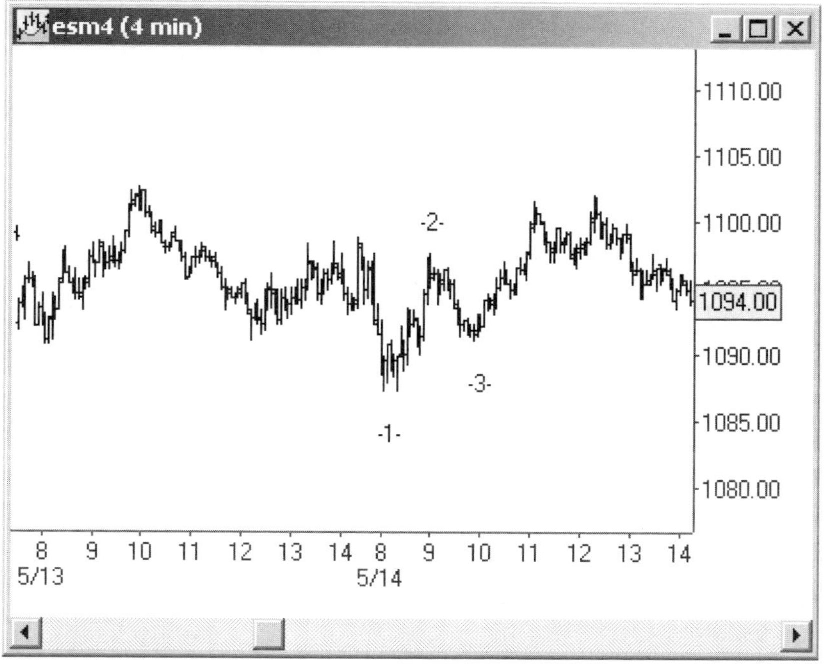

In this method, we will size the vortex pattern as before, but using a different placement technique. In the chart above, I've marked three different swings. In our standard method of sizing the vortex, we would put the center on Point 3, a spiral on Point 2, and a spoke on Point 1. The purpose for this is to find a vortex that is vibrating in harmony with the market. Just as it takes at least three points to really fit a circle to price, we also need three points to fit our vortex to price. But there's really no reason for us to use this particular order. We can fit our vortex using any combination of spirals and spoke that we choose. In theory, if the vortex really is a governing pattern, all correct fittings should have some effect on the market.

So here's an example of how to switch this up:

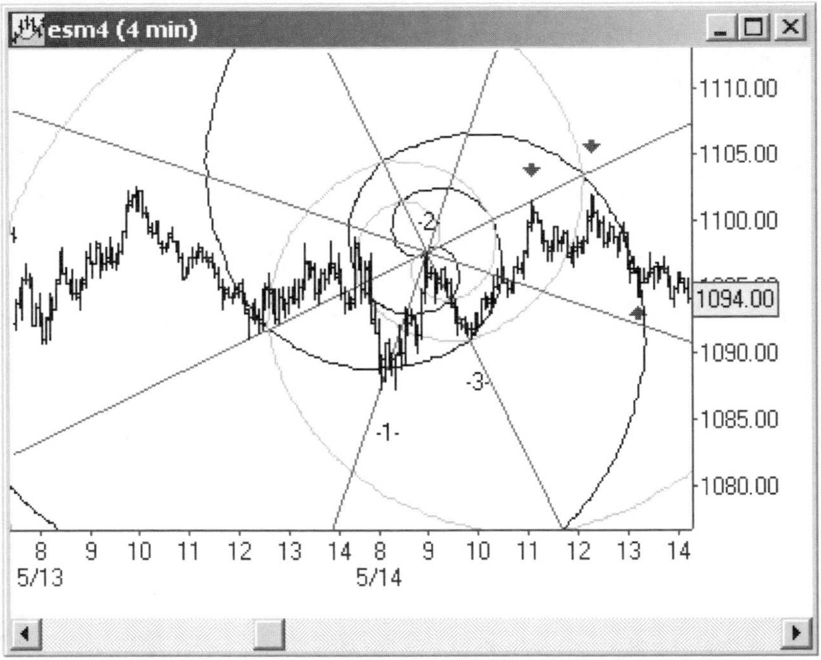

In this case, I've centered the vortex on Point 2, not Point 3. The spiral now goes through Point 3, but the spoke remains fixed on Point 1. You can see how well this pattern described the price action after Point 3 came in. I've marked important turns with arrows. We got both the highs, as shown by the first two arrows, and then price slid neatly down the dark spiral into the third arrow before breaking out of the pattern to the right.

Method 2: Pure Spirals

In this approach, we get rid of the spokes all together, and just use the spirals themselves.

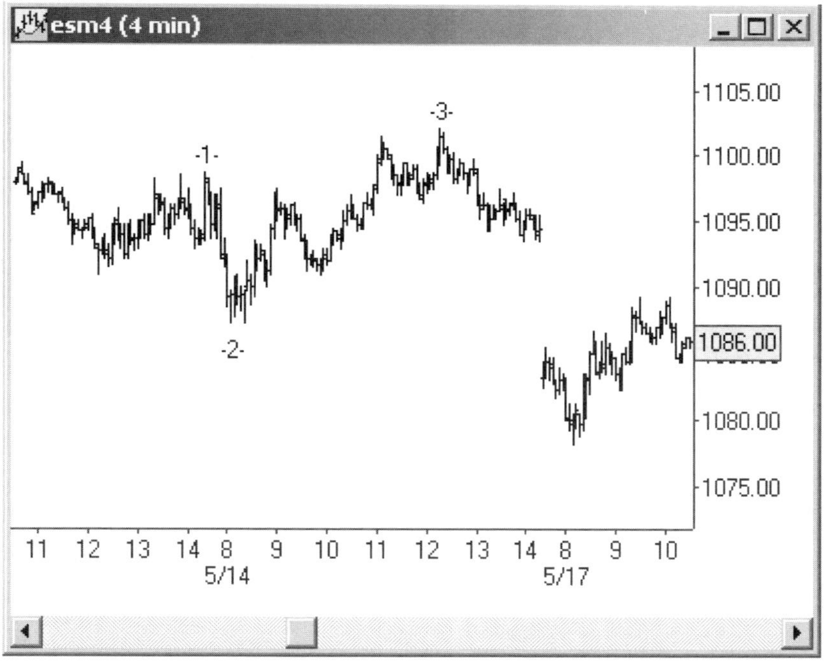

So in the chart above, what we want to do is place the vortex on Point 3 as usual, but this time try and get a spiral to fall through both Points 1 and 2. You can't always use this method, because sometimes you just can't find a way to get a spiral to fit, but other times it's very easy. So it's a hit and miss kind of approach, but does warrant some further investigation. If you can get a single spiral travelling through three points on your chart, you know you've found a good vortex fit. Here's one that I found on the above chart:

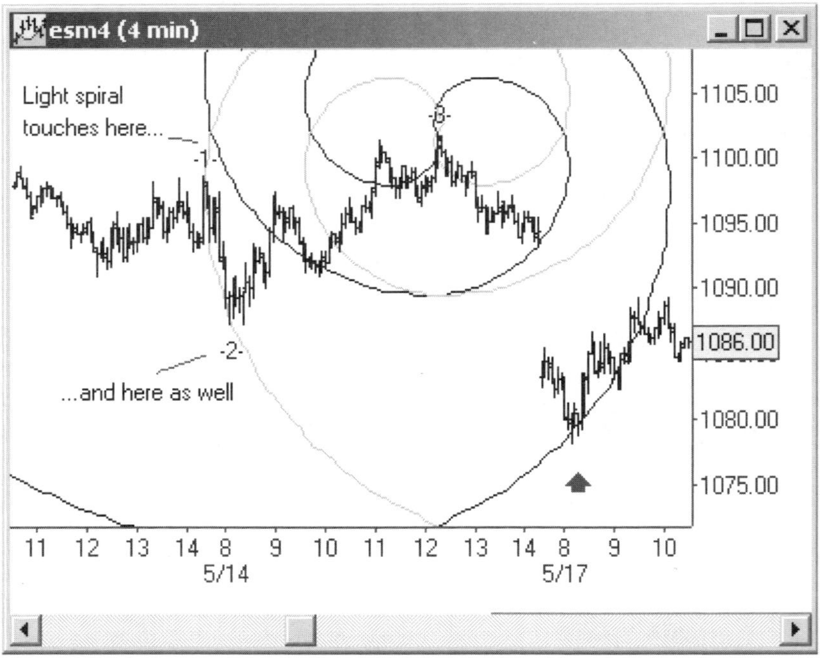

So we have the light spiral starting off at Point 3, and bending back to pass through both Points 1 and 2. The dark spiral ended up catching the low on the 17th, as well as the final bar on the 14th before the gap down.

One nice thing about using this kind of approach is that you don't have a vortex pair anymore. The fit is based totally on that one spiral passing through key points, so for the vortex to work properly you've got to keep it there. I feel the spokes are still valid, although I've chosen to leave them off of the chart in this example.

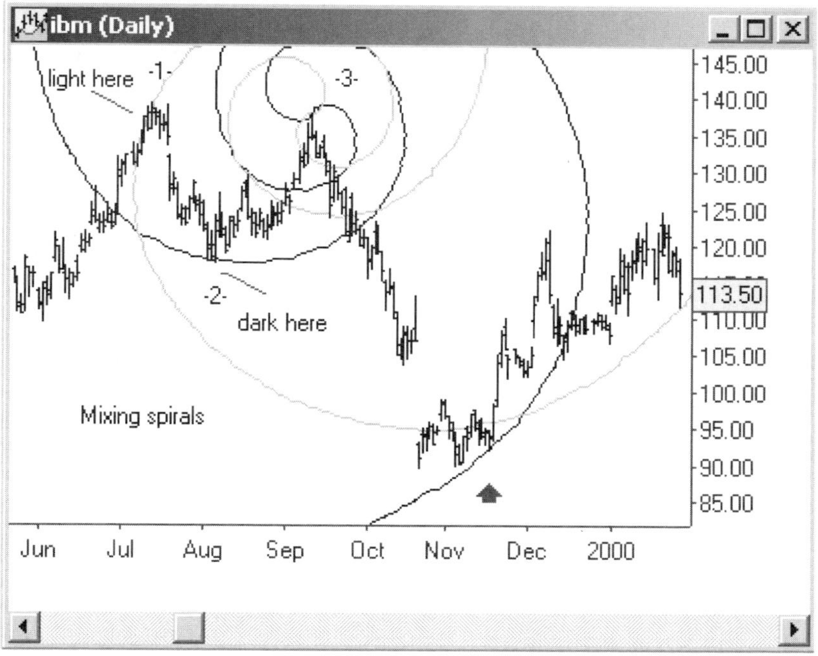

Here's a variation on the idea. In this case, we are mixing spirals on Points 1 and 2. So we place our Vortex on Point 3 as usual, and require spirals at Points 1 and 2, but they don't have to be the same colors.

So on the chart above, we have a light spiral passing through Point 1, and a dark spiral passing through Point 2. These are usually easier to find than the ones with the same spiral going through both of the first two points, although there are times when it can be tough as well. Like the previous example, you usually don't need to make use of the vortex pair with this kind of sizing.

On the chart above, IBM dropped hard until it touched the dark spiral, which then set up a nice rally to recover a lot of what had been lost on the way down.

These are the kinds of approaches that I was working with when I first started applying these patterns to the market. They work, and should be investigated by all serious students of the market.

Method 3: As a Floating Overlay

This method is a little tougher to apply, but has been used with great success by a number of traders I know who have been playing with these tools since Wave59's beta testing days. It requires a lot of pattern matching, and is a very discretionary kind of approach.

In this method, you use the vortex as a pattern that doesn't require any fixed points. So there is no Point 1, 2, and 3. What you try to do is place the vortex in such a way that it describes a large chunk of recent market history. The center of the pattern is oftentimes floating out in space in these cases, so there isn't a right or wrong spot to place it.

The spokes become very important in this kind of approach, and are used extensively in locating the center point.

Let's look at an example:

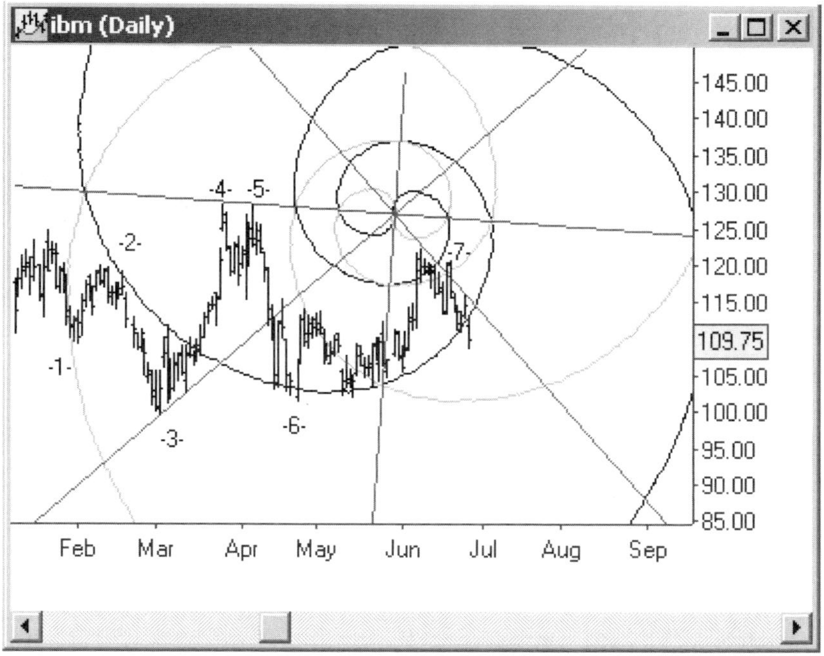

The first thing you'll notice about this vortex is that the center is not at a swing point. It's actually just floating out in space. That's a fairly standard characteristic of this approach. In placing this pattern, I've tried to find as may price hits along spirals and spokes as I possibly could. These are marked on the chart above.

The low at Point 1 came in on a spiral, as did the high at Point 2. Point 3 bottomed along a spoke, then experienced resistance at the dark spiral on the way up to Points 4 and 5, both of which were stopped in their tracks by another spoke. Point 6 bottomed along a spiral, which supported price for a month and half before the rally up to Point 7, which occurred at a spoke. At the time this vortex was fit, the market was sliding down this spoke from Point 7.

So what we have is a vortex pattern that the market is following very closely. It's an extremely tight fit, because it describes practically everything that has happened the last 6 months. Now that we've located this pattern, we can use it to forecast future turns as well. Something that the market is following so closely should continue to provide useful timing information until price breaks free by moving far enough to the right. Here's what ended up happening:

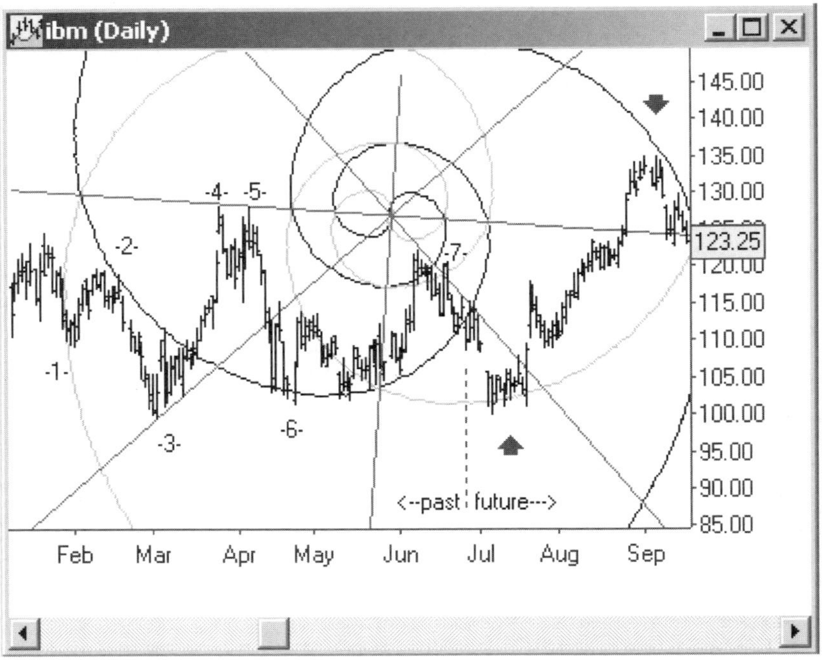

The two arrows show the turning points that this method caught. That second arrow turned out to be the high before a 50 point drop occurred, so this vortex was really locked into the market rhythm.

This method oftentimes produces stunning charts, although you do have to play around with the tool quite a bit to find where the vortex center is. Because of this, it makes it a little tough to use when daytrading short time frames.

Method 4: Simplified Overlay

I've also seen the overlay approach used in a simplified way that also works well. In this technique, you disallow rotating or enlarging the vortex pattern. The idea is that every market contains important swing numbers that are built into the vortex itself. Once a chart is properly scaled, the vortex simply needs to be placed near swing termination points and you'll get a whole slew of important support and resistance numbers for the future.

Like the more complicated version we just discussed, this method doesn't require the center of the vortex to be located on price. Here's an example:

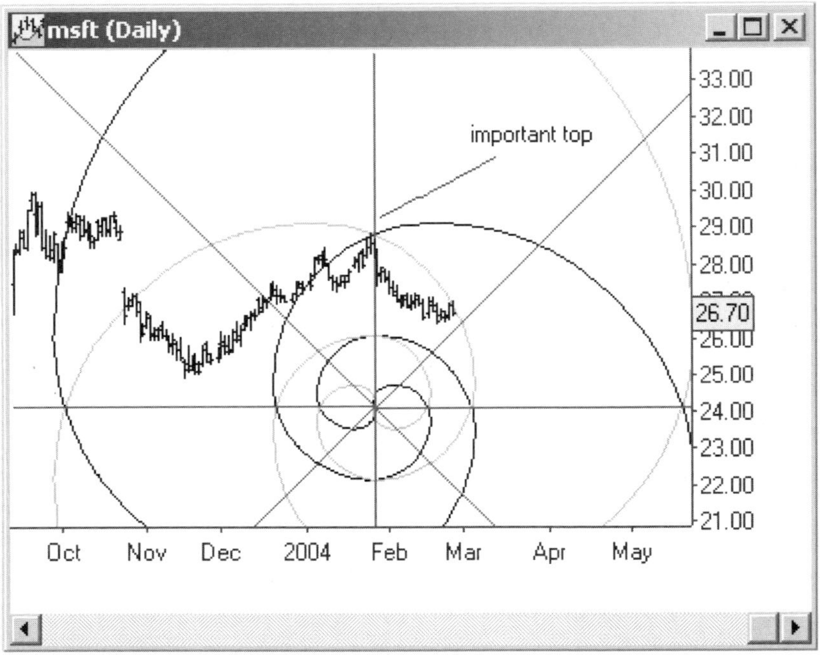

In the chart above, MSFT has formed an important swing high. To get support levels on the way down, we place the vortex so the center is located at the same bar as the top, but offset below so that the spirals touch the high instead of the center. Now, on the way down, price should find support at the spirals and spokes provided by this vortex.

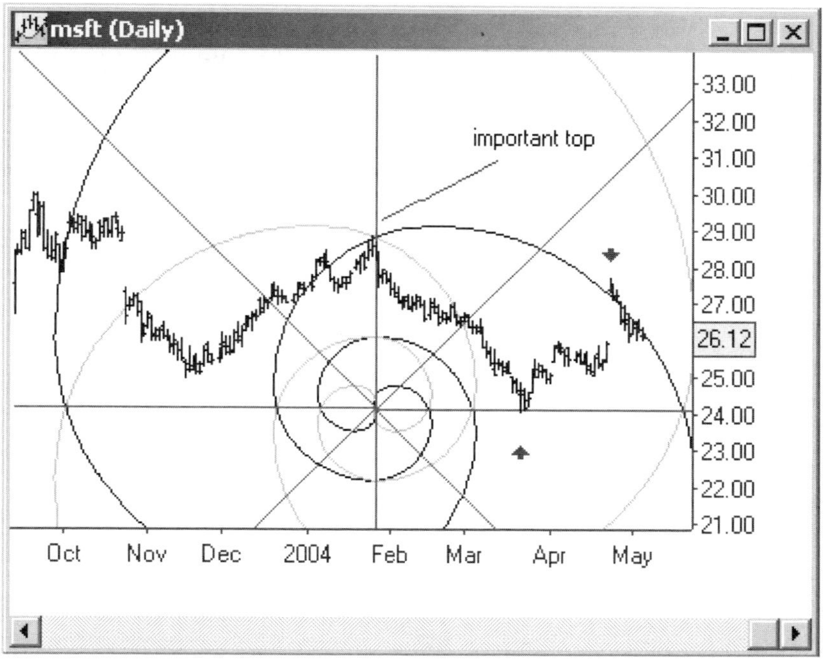

Price bounced off the horizontal spoke, and rallied up to the dark spiral. This is probably the simplest method for applying the vortex, but scaling is critical.

The trader who told me about using the vortex in this way has been so successful with it that he has started a trading fund and advisory service based upon this approach. If you'd like to check him out, visit the resources page at wave59.com for contact information.

So we've discussed four different approaches in this chapter, but there are many more methods that could be used. After you master the standard approach as discussed in the bulk of this book, I suggest experimenting with some of these methods. It's definitely worth a bit of study to see how many different ways the market expresses itself along the guidelines set out by the Fibonacci Vortex pattern. Just remember to scale your charts!

CHAPTER 12:
Conclusion

You should now have a complete understanding of what the vortex is about, how to apply it to your charts, and how to use it to forecast future support and resistance levels. It's not an easy tool to learn, but isn't rocket science either. All that you need now is to practice.

The easiest way to apply this is to let the computer draw the pattern for you, as well as handle all chart scaling calculations. There's only one program that can do this, and that's the one I wrote specifically for the job. You can learn more about it by visiting *www.wave59.com* . It's also got some great confirming indicators, some of which you've seen in Chapter 10. I wrote Wave59, so maybe I'm a little biased towards it, but even if I wasn't the developer I'd still be recommending it. You should definitely take a look at the 30 day trial.

If you are already happy with your trading software, or like to do things the old-fashioned way by hand, what you'll need to do is get a hold of some clear plastic overlays. You can find them in any office supply store for use with overhead projectors. Then, construct a set of about 10 vortex patterns in increasing size.

You start off by creating a golden spiral, using a ruler and compass. Review chapter one for directions on how to go about doing this. Once you have that one spiral, you can flip and rotate it to get all the others you need for your pattern. Draw the vortex onto one of your clear plastic sheets, and mark the size up in the corner. The smallest one can be 1, with the next larger being 2, and all the way up.

Once you have your sheets made, you are ready to apply the vortex to your charts. If you've got a standard charting program, you'll need to find a way to scale your charts. Back when I used to use TradeStation, I would measure out my chart with a ruler to make sure it was a perfect square on the screen. I would then set it to show exactly one day of price action, then force the high and the low to conform to my scale using manual scaling options. It was a pain in the rear, no doubt, but it got me a properly scaled chart in the end.

At that point, you just have to hold your patterns up to the screen, and go through the sizing routine. If this sounds like it would be too much trouble to use in real time, keep in mind that I used to trade this way for years on a 5 minute chart. By the end of the day, your arm will be a little tired, but the extra clarity that the vortex brings is more than worth it. Of course, after a few months of that, you'll be ready to go and program your own charting package to do this properly, which is the same thing that happened to me…

After you find 30 or so vortex patterns, you should be ready to go in the real world. This pattern is the grandfather of the standard approaches used today, and gives so much more depth of information that you'll never want to go back to your old methods once you've tried the vortex for a few days. Give it fair shake, and I'm sure you'll agree.

I hope you've enjoyed this book. It was fun to write, as I love talking about the vortex. One of the best things about writing trading books is to hear back from readers who have successfully put the techniques to use in their own trading. It's even better when they share the new twists that they have put on the tools to customize them. So if you end up incorporating this tool into your own trading, please drop me a line sometime and tell me how things are going. Don't be shy!

Thanks for reading, good luck, and happy trading!

All charts in this book were created using the Wave59 RT trading software. For more information, or to contact the author, please visit www.wave59.com.

Notes:

Notes:

Notes: